PHYSICS FOR

DOGS

A CRASH COURSE IN CATCHING CATS, FRISBEES, AND CARS

PHYSICS FOR DOGS

A CRASH COURSE IN CATCHING CATS, FRISBEES, AND CARS

JOHN-ANDREW SANDBROOK AND **DARA FLYNN, MS**

Technical edit by **CAROLANN KOLECI, PhD**

Foreword by **PEPPER SANDBROOK-FLYNN, PhD**

Published by
Adams Media, a division of F+W Media, Inc.
57 Littlefield Street, Avon, MA 02322. U.S.A.
www.adamsmedia.com

ISBN 10: 1-4405-1009-1
ISBN 13: 978-1-4405-1009-0
eISBN 10: 1-4405-1109-8
eISBN 13: 978-1-4405-1109-7

Printed in the United States of America.

10 9 8 7 6 5 4 3 2 1

Library of Congress Cataloging-in-Publication Data
is available from the publisher.

This publication is designed to provide accurate and authoritative information with regard to the subject matter covered. It is sold with the understanding that the publisher is not engaged in rendering legal, accounting, or other professional advice. If legal advice or other expert assistance is required, the services of a competent professional person should be sought.
—From a *Declaration of Principles* jointly adopted by a Committee of the American Bar Association and a Committee of Publishers and Associations

Many of the designations used by manufacturers and sellers to distinguish their product are claimed as trademarks. Where those designations appear in this book and Adams Media was aware of a trademark claim, the designations have been printed with initial capital letters.

No humans were harmed in the making of this book. Please consult your veterinarian before engaging in these activities.

Illustrations by Eric Andrews.

*This book is available at quantity discounts for bulk purchases.
For information, please call 1-800-289-0963.*

Dedication

To my loving sisters . . . and mass-less, frictionless ropes. —JAS

To Cleo, Dusty, Gretchen, Gucci, and Kip: Without you, we would never have seen the math of mayhem or purpose in playtime. —the Authors

CONTENTS

Acknowledgments

To our editor Victoria Sandbrook and everyone at Adams Media, for your hard work and insight.

Foreword

Eat. Sleep. Bark. Poop. Eat. Sleep. Bark. Poop.

It's not hard to keep track of the pattern of many dogs' lives. What else is there to do when you have every comfort at your paws and lack the inspiration and means to achieve great things?

Since the dawn of domestication, humans have created an inverse proportion between the praise we get and the prominence of our wild sides. Don't pretend you haven't noticed. The longer we sit pretty, the more biscuits we get. The longer we bark at the shadows (even the ones that are obviously malevolent), the longer we have to sit in our crates and whine our miserable apologies. To some breeds, a life of sweaters and paw-polish is enough. To others, the desire for more presses dogs like myself to seek out change.

At this stage in evolution, it would be foolhardy to suggest a revolt and beyond ridiculous—for many of us—to dream of setting out on our own. Can you imagine a wild pack of formerly well-trained Corgis staring down a moose in a northern wilderness? We'd all love to believe ourselves cunning enough to resume predatory status over game larger than Fluffy from next door, but the biology of centuries of breeding simply makes a return to the wild improbable.

Luckily, ours is not a dichotomous world. We don't need to make a choice between our ancient instincts and our comfortable couches if we take the time to understand the world we're living in and apply the old ways to the new. Our wolf ancestors may not have known a rabbit from a radian, but they knew how to make the world work the way they wanted it to. With the collective knowledge of thousands of dogs, the ground-breaking scholarship of these soon-to-be-renowned authors, and a bit of studying, we dogs of all breeds and backgrounds can stop taking chances and making valiant attempts at achievement. With physics, we can find purpose in everything.

If you don't believe me, just attend an agility competition. Dogs of all shapes and sizes manage to take on obstacles that contradict the lessons of our household lives and take us back to the skills we would have needed in the fields and forests of old. They leap onto, jump over, climb up, run through, and balance on obstacles that dare them to fail. And if you asked, you'd find that most of them were afraid of one challenge or another when they first arrived in the yard. But with practice, they grew to be some of the most confident and daring pooches you'll meet.

Little do most of them know that their success is dependent on laws, theorems, and formulas they could apply to just about anything! Canine physics mastery combines the self-assurance you get from having a job and the pride you'll feel when you realize you're really good at what you do. You may not have prey to hunt, but you almost certainly have a kitchen to prowl. You may not have game to run down, but you've got cats and squirrels and bicycles and cars and cats and children and toys and cats. And though you've no cave to make your own, you're probably even more grateful for having an owner on whom you can rely and furniture on which you can shed. Canine physics gives you the benefits of the wild in the comfort of your own home. It's like having a bone and eating it, too.

This book is divided into sections that will allow you to progress from behavior you currently exhibit through new skills and tactics, all the way through the feats of greatness you've only dreamed of accomplishing. Each unit focuses on a single action, though you'll quickly learn that there's more than one way to . . . well, do just about anything to that poor cat!

Please remember that there's no responsible way to put yourself in danger. Consult a qualified veterinarian before attempting more physical activity than you're used to and seek professional agility, obedience, and skill training before you attempt to emulate new, challenging behaviors. This book intends to offer academic mastery of the objective facts behind the feats; the experienced professionals in your life are the only ones qualified to decide whether the advanced practice of canine physics is right for you.

I wish you all the best in your happier, more mathematically sound existence!

—Pepper Sandbrook-Flynn, PhD

LESSONS IN THIS CHAPTER

EATING AND DRINKING

Dogs love to eat, but for centuries after domestication, only the most cunning curs have made off with choice prey from their masters' tables. Add vectors, speed, and force to your natural abilities to make finding food a game of skill, not luck.

ED-1. GET FOOD OFF THE COUNTER

No food is as tempting as the food you can reach but aren't allowed to have. Even under your human's nose, the snatch-and-run technique you've tried so many times *can* be successful—but only if you carefully observe your surroundings and properly calculate your approach.

First, calculate the time it will take for the human to intercept you (t_{total}).

$$\beta = distance\ human\ must\ travel\ to\ intercept\ you = 3m$$

$$t_{react} = time\ until\ human\ reacts = 0.28s$$

$$s_h = human's\ speed\ 0.962\frac{m}{s}$$

$$t_{travel} = \frac{d_h}{s_h} = \frac{3}{0.962\frac{m}{s}} = 3.12s$$

$$t_{total} = t_{travel} + t_{react} = 3.12s + 0.28s = 3.14s$$

Now calculate your confidence in your success (y) when you account for the following variables.

$$\lambda = your\ horizontal\ distance\ to\ food = 2m$$

$$\Delta = your\ speed = 1\frac{m}{s}$$

$$\Sigma = food's\ Taste\ Factor = 1.8$$

$$\theta = your\ angle\ to\ food = 55°$$

$$\eta = chance\ human\ will\ not\ react = .02$$

$$y = \frac{\Sigma\left(t_{total} - \frac{\lambda}{\Delta}\right)}{\frac{\cos\theta}{\eta}} = \frac{1.8\left(3.14s - \frac{2m}{1\frac{m}{s}}\right)}{\frac{.022}{.02}} = 1.86$$

The food's Taste Factor is a strong motivator to take the chance with strong confidence in your ability to get the food before you get caught. Go for it!

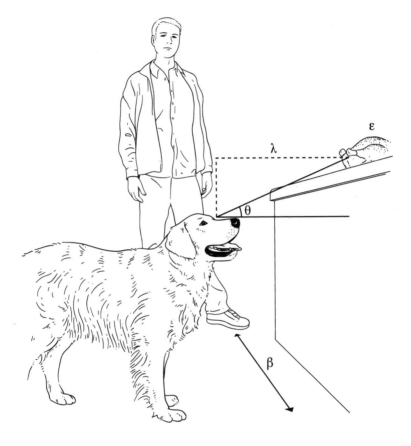

Fig. 1. Dog carefully considers confidence in classic snatch-and-run tactic.

ED-2. GET FOOD OFF THE TABLE
PART I: THE SNEAK ATTACK

Assuming you are at coordinate (0, 0, 0), the unit vector describing the direction of attack is

$$\frac{(d_x, d_y, d_z)}{\|(d_x, d_y, d_z)\|}$$

d_x, d_y, d_z: distance to food in each special dimension

θ: Angle to food from the xy plane

$d_x = 0.4$ $\qquad$ d_y: 0.8 $\qquad$ $\theta = 40°$ $\qquad$ d_z: Unknown

To determine d_z, use the angle θ, d_x, and d_y.

$$d_z = \tan\theta \sqrt{d_x^2 + d_y^2}$$

$$d_z = \tan 40° \sqrt{(.4m)^2 + (0.8m)^2}$$

$$d_z = 0.84\sqrt{.16m^2 + .64m^2} = 0.84m \times 0.89m = 0.75m$$

Then, the unit vector in the direction of the food becomes,

$$\frac{(0.4,\ 0.8,\ .075)}{\sqrt{(0.4)^2 + (0.8)^2 + (0.75)^2}}$$

$$\frac{(0.4,\ 0.8,\ 0.75)}{1.36} = (0.29, 0.59, 0.55)$$

Force must be applied in this direction over the length of the original vector (1.36m) in order to steal the food. Care must be taken to ensure this distance is as short as possible allowing for a quick retreat in either the d_x or d_y directions (under the chair or under the table respectively).

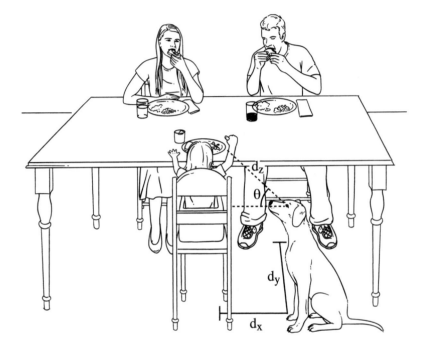

Fig. 2. Dog isolates likely target, identifies attack vectors, and prepares retreat paths.

ED-3. GET FOOD OFF THE TABLE
PART II: THE DISTRACTION

Assume starting location has coordinates (0, 0, 0).

First vector of motion must be in the direction of cat, with sufficient magnitude to be scary enough that humans will leave table for chase.

$$d_1 = (-1.5, 1.4, 0)$$

$$\|d_1\| = \sqrt{(-1.5)^2 + 1.4^2 + 0^2} = 2.05m$$

Change direction into path d_2; speed up to start run back to table by applying vector (1.5, 2, 0).

$$d_2 = d_1 + (1.5, 2, 0) = (-1.5 + 1.5, 1.4 + 2, 0 + 0) = (0, 3.4, 0)$$

$$\| d_2 \| = 3.4m$$

Keep speed going around corner but change directions completely from y to x.

$$d_3 = d_2 + (3.4, -3.4, 0) = (3.4, 0, 0)$$

Another 90° turn returns you to the dining room, but slow slightly to prepare for dinner.

$$d_4 = d_3 + (-3.4, 3, 0) = (0, 3, 0)$$

Cut the corner by turning before 90° to ensure arrival before humans get back.

$$d_5 = d_4 + (-2.5, -1.8, 0) = (-2.5, 1.2, 0)$$

Prepare for transition into the z-axis for jump. Vector to land on table is as follows

$$d_6 = d_5 + (2, -.6, 3) = (-.5, .6, 3)$$

Enjoy dinner! Final vector values for units traveled:

$$d_1 = (-1.5, 1.4, 0) \qquad d_2 = (0, 3.4, 0) \qquad d_3 = (3.4, 0, 0)$$

$$d_4 = (0, 3, 0) \qquad d_5 = (-2.5, 1.2, 0) \qquad d_6 = (-.5, .6, 3)$$

Watch for humans racing around corner. Suggestions for maximum food consumption include:

Increase magnitude by a greater amount along d_3

Cut the corner between d_4 and d_5 earlier

Cause cat to knock over expensive vase or books so humans chase it instead of you

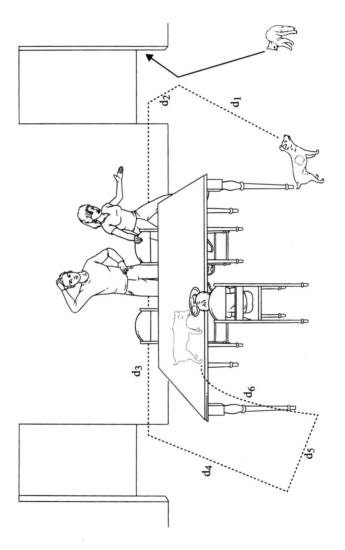

Fig. 3. Dog utilizes surroundings to create and take advantage of mayhem.

ED-4. GET INTO THE GARBAGE CAN

Calculate the force needed to open the garbage can's lid (moving lid from A to B on path d).

r: radius of lid's path s: speed at which lid will open

t: how long it takes to open the lid d: distance travelled by the tip of lid

$$s = \frac{d}{t}$$

$$d = \frac{90°}{360°} \times 2\pi r$$

$$d = \frac{1}{4} \times 2\pi \times 0.25\ m = 0.39\ m$$

$$s = \frac{0.39\ m}{2\ s} = 0.195\ \frac{m}{s}$$

Given this velocity, the lid obtains a circular acceleration of:

$$a = \frac{s^2}{r}$$

$$a = \frac{0.195^2\ \frac{m^2}{s^2}}{0.25m} = 0.15\ \frac{m}{s^2}$$

The average garbage can lid is approximately 0.113kg. Therefore, the force needed to lift the lid

is

$$F = 0.113 kg \times 0.15\ \frac{m}{s^2} = .02\ N$$

Given the garbage can's dimensions this may or may not be a worthwhile endeavor. If volume is

greater than 5.5m³, use time and effort to open the lid. Otherwise, wait until bigger garbage can

is found.

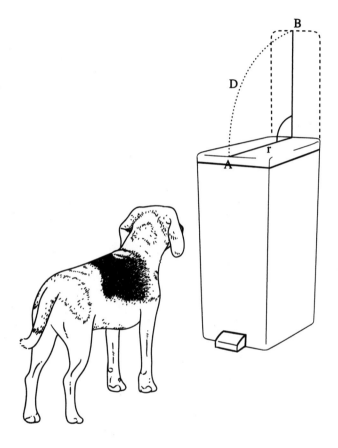

Fig. 4. Dog analyzes value of passive target in terms of work and volume.

ED-5. GET INTO A CABINET (LOW)

To open this cabinet door (with dimensions 0.9m high by 0.76m wide), apply a force slightly past

equilibrium. In this case, equilibrium will occur when you exert half your weight.

First, calculate the magnitude of the force opposing motion. Your mass is 15kg.

$$F_{dog} = mg = 15kg \times 9.81 \frac{m}{s^2} = 147.15N$$

The opposing force is acting at midpoint of door, that is, 0.45m from hinge.

Exert counter-clockwise force at 30° angle (θ) to door, 0.85m from hinge. Effective normal force

being applied on door is given by:

$$F_{eff} = F_{dog} \sin \theta = 147.15N \times \sin 30 = 73.575N$$

Torque created by F_eff:

$$T_{dog} = F_{eff} D_{eff} = 73.575 \ N \times 0.85 \ m = 62.54Nm$$

For equilibrium, restoring torque must equal moment created by dog. Therefore:

$$T_{restore} = T_{dog}$$

$$F_{restore} D_{restore} = 62.54N$$

$$F_{restore} = \frac{62.54 \ Nm}{0.45 \ m} = 139N$$

Fig. 5. Dog calculates equilibrium, angle, force, and torque to nab protected treats.

ED-6. GET INTO A CABINET (HIGH)

You must travel $0.4m$ (d) and jump $0.91m$ (h) to steal treats from a high cabinet. Assume your

normal jumping force is 1.5 times the force of gravity.

$$F_j = 1.5mg$$

When tempted with the opportunity for stolen treats, the Treat Motivator of 0.3 is factored into

the equation.

$$F_t = F_j + 0.3mg = 1.5mg + 0.3mg = 1.8mg$$

The y-direction acceleration due to this force is $a = 1.8g$.

You must start at a run to make up the x-direction distance. In a small kitchen, assume you reach

a top speed of 3.5 m/s.

In the y-direction, to find your speed reached, assume you start at rest in the y-

direction and the total jumping force is applied in a quarter second.

$$V_y = V_{ay} + at = 0 + 1.8\frac{m}{s} \times 9.81\frac{m}{s} \times 0.25\frac{m}{s} = 4.415\frac{m}{s}$$

Use this as the starting velocity in the y-direction, calculate time of jump

$$\acute{V_y} = V_y - gt$$

$$-4.415\frac{m}{s} = -9.81\frac{m}{s} \times t$$

$$t = 0.45\ s$$

Use this time to calculate Δy

$$\Delta y = V_{ay}t - \frac{1}{2}gt^2$$

$$\Delta y = 4.415\frac{m}{s} \times 0.45s - \frac{1}{2} \times 9.81\frac{m}{s} \times 0.45s^2$$

$$\Delta y = 0.993m$$

Use t=0.45s to calculate Δx. Assume constant velocity in the x-direction.

$$\Delta x = 3.5m - 0.45m = 1.575m$$

Since $\Delta y > h$ and $\Delta x > d$, you get the treats!

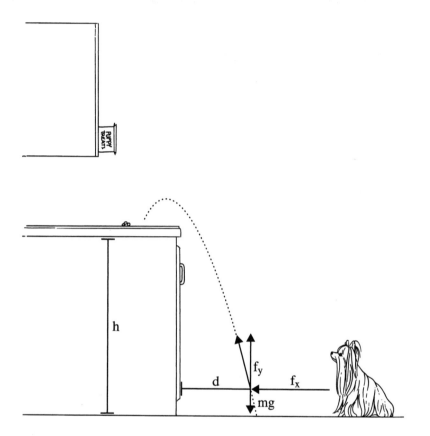

Fig. 6. Dog accounts for visible treats' impact on abilities.

ED-7. GET INTO YOUR KIBBLE CONTAINER

You have to overcome the break strength of the paper bag containing the kibble.

Using your teeth, try to pull a corner off of the bag. To overcome the yield strength, you have to apply a large enough force per unit area.

$$\sigma = \frac{F}{A_o}$$

The cross-sectional area of the corner of the bag is calculated from a 45-45-90 triangle of the top corner.

$$A_o = 2 \times b \times t$$

$$b = base\ of\ triangle = 15cm = 0.15m$$

$$t = thickness\ of\ paper = 2mm = 0.002m$$

$$A = 6 \times 10^{-4} m^2$$

Assume, normally, you can apply a puling force equal to ⅛ your mass.

$$F = \frac{m_{dog}g}{4} = \frac{32kg \times 9.81\frac{m}{s^2}}{8} = 39.24N$$

$$\sigma_{dog} = \frac{3.924N}{6 \times 10^{-4}} = 65.4kPa$$

Assume the yield strength of the dry bag is

$$\sigma_{y_{bag}} = 100kpa$$

If you continue attempting to tear the bag, you will find out that the strength of the bag decreases proportionally with the increasing wetness of the bag. Stand over the bag, think about your Krunchies, and let drool soak the bag to the point that the yield strength lowers to 64.8kPa. Because

$$65.4kPa > 64.8kpa$$

you get your Krunchies!

Fig. 7. Dog learns impact of slobber moisture on yield strength.

ED-8. GET INTO THE FRIDGE

After the trash can, there is no greater food storage fortress than the refrigerator. Completing

this task takes a dog who can make the most of the tools humans don't expect you to use.

One way to open the refrigerator door is by pulling on a dish towel hanging from the handle.

Assuming a frictionless hinge and a simplified refrigerator design, we can calculate the mass of

the refrigerator door.

$$m_{fridge} = 260 \; lbs = 118 \; kg$$

$$m_{door} = \frac{2}{3}\left(\frac{1}{5}m_{fridge}\right) = \frac{2 \times 118 \; kg}{15} = 15.73 \; kg$$

The force from the seal of the door is 45N ($\cong$ 10 lbs-f, assumed applied on the door handle). You

must also move the weight of the door. Total force needed in the x-direction is:

$$F_{tot}^x = F_{seal} + F_{door}$$

$$F_{tot}^x = 45 \; N + 15.73 \; kg \times 9.81 \frac{m}{s^2} = 199.34 \; N$$

Pull the door at an angle of 40° from the horizontal. Approximate your pull strength of to be 1.5

times its' weight and include the slip of your feet on the kitchen floor (assume an unfinished

wooden floor) to find your total pull force.

$$\mu = 0.5 \quad m_{dog} = 29.5 \; kg$$

$$F_{lab} = 1.5 \; m_{dog}g = 1.5 \times 29.5 \; kg \times 9.81 \frac{m}{s^2} = 434.10 \; N$$

$$F_f = \mu \, m_{dog}g = 0.5 \times 29.5 \; kg \times 9.81 \frac{m}{s^2} = 144.69 \; N$$

$$F_{pull} = F_{dog} - F_f = 434.10 \; N - 144.69 \; N = 289.40 \; N$$

Now determine the x component of the applied force; compare to the x-direction force.

$$F_{pull}^x = F_{pull} \cos 40° = 289.40 \; N \times 0.766 = 221.69 \; N$$

$$F_{pull}^x = 221.69 \; N > F_{tot}^x = 199.34 \; N$$

Success!

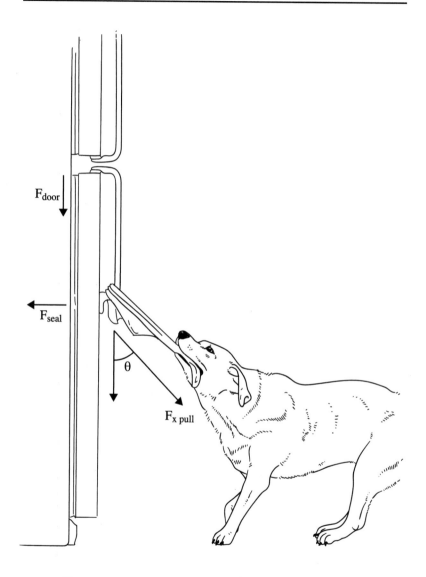

Fig. 8. Dog tackles food fortress with knowledge of force and friction.

ED-9. DRINK OUT OF THE TOILET

Before drinking toilet water, you must understand the magnitude of risk involved.

Typical polypropylene toilet seat specifications help us find the seat's mass (m).

$$density = 0.946 \, \frac{g}{cm^3}$$

$$volume = 3032cm^3$$

$$m = density \times volume = 0.946 \, \frac{g}{cm^3} \times 3032cm^3 = 2.87kg$$

Should the seat fall, its angular momentum, L, can be determined by the following formula.

$$L = msrsin\theta$$

where s is the lid's speed, r is the lid's length, and θ is the angle between the lid and it's

direction of movement. The seat will fall 61 cm (d) over 2s (t). Since the lid is always moving

perpendicular to itself (90°), sinθ is 1, simplifying the equation to,

$$L = msr$$

$$L = (2.87kg)\left(\frac{0.61m}{2s}\right)(0.43m) = .376\frac{kgm^2}{s}$$

The lid will undergo acceleration only from the component of gravity perpendicular to itself.

Assuming vertical is 0°, this component is represented by,

$$\frac{d^2x}{dt^2} = g \, \cos\theta$$

Assuming the lid falls from an initial position of 0° and your head is approximately 6 inches tall,

you can calculate how many degrees the seat will fall.

$$\tan(90 - \theta_{fall}) = \frac{\text{height of head}}{\text{length of lid}} = \frac{0.13m}{0.43m}$$

$$\theta_{fall} = 73.18°$$

All calculations prove that a falling toilet seat will hurt and likely create a noise enough to draw

attention to you. Neither consequence serves you well, so take care.

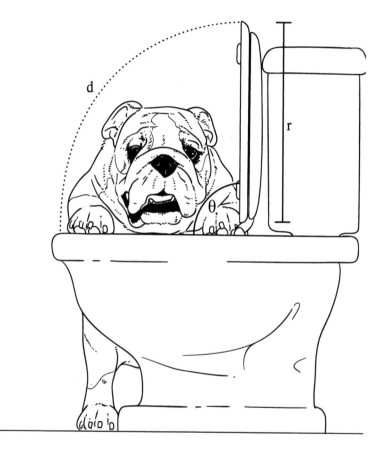

Fig. 9. Dog analyzes possible risks of injury due to angular
momentum of falling toilet seat.

ED-10. DRINK OUT OF THE FISH TANK

Placing your paws on the tank to drink creates a risk of pushing the tank off its table. You must ensure that drinking from the tank will not damage it, the fish, or you. To do so, find the weight needed to move a full tank.

First, find the force of static friction keeping the tank in place, where μ is the coefficient of friction between the table and the tank and n is the normal force exerted by the tank (with mass of m, weighed down by gravity of g) on the table.

$$F_f = \mu n = \mu(mg)$$

Assuming the table is metal and the tank is glass with the table aligned perfectly horizontally,

$$F_f = 0.6 \times m \times g$$

$$m = (w \times d \times h)997\frac{kg}{m^3}$$

$$m = (1m \times 0.5m \times 0.75m)997\frac{kg}{m^3}$$

$$m = .375m^3 \times 997\frac{kg}{m^3} = 373.88kg$$

$$F_f = .6 \times 373.88kg \times 9.81\frac{m}{s^2} = 2200.66N$$

If you only lean on the tank, you would need to weigh approximately 224.33kg (493.52lb) to push the tank off the table. This is significantly more than the average dog weighs however, smaller tanks can lower this value rapidly so use caution.

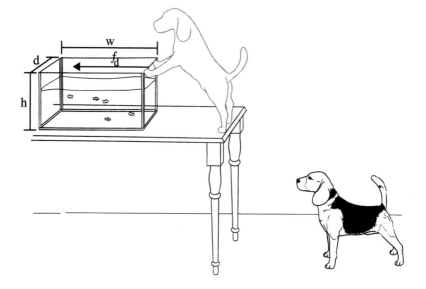

Fig. 10. Dog calculates likelihood that favorite water reservoir will withstand weight.

ED-11. EAT YOUR OWN POOP

You know everything you need to about your own poop: it smells good and your human doesn't want you to have it. Could anything be more appealing? Next time your human holds you back, calculate the force necessary to overcome the force of gravity on your human. Let R be $(0m, 0m)$.

$$C_g = (-0.1m, 1.13m)$$

$$S = (0.12m, 1.6m)$$

$$m_h = 90.7kg$$

$$\tau = Fl$$

$$\tau_{C_g} = 90.7kg \times 9.81\frac{m^2}{s^2} \times 1.13m = 1005.44Nm \; (+)$$

$$\tau_s = F_x s_x + F_y s_y = F \sin \alpha \, s_x + F \cos \alpha \, s_y$$

$$= F \sin 35 \times 0.12 + F \cos 35 \times 1.6$$

$$= (0.07 + 1.31)F = 1.38F$$

When $\tau_s > \tau_{C_g}$ human will fall.

Let $\tau_s = \tau_{C_g}$ to find F.

$$1.38F = 1005.44$$

$$F = 728.58N$$

Normal pulling force is equal to twice your mass force

$$F_{norm} = 2m_{dog}g = 2 \times 6.80 \times 9.81 = 133.49N$$

Factor in the Treat Strength Multiplier, which is equal to 5.5 times your normal pulling strength and you get

$$F_{total} = 5.5 \times 133.49N = 734.19N$$

You have to muster all your strength to get it.

Fig. 11. Dog uses element of surprise and pulling force to partake in taboo treat.

ED-12. EAT SOMEONE ELSE'S POOP

While your own poop is tempting, other dogs' poop is a delicacy. In this way, poop is much like

grass. Calculate the angle (θ) at which you'll need to jump and range (R) needed to make it into

the other yard. To be cautious, add 0.1m to the height to assure clearance (h_{max} = 1.6m). Let u

be your initial velocity.

$$h_{max} = \frac{u^2(\sin\theta)^2}{2g}$$

Assume ideal conditions and account for the following acceleration quantities:

$$horizontal\ acceleration = 0\frac{m}{s^2} \qquad vertical\ acceleration = -9.81\frac{m}{s^2}$$

Your approach for the jump may vary, depending on breed and excitement. For the purpose of

this calculation, the horizontal component velocity is 5m/s.

$$u\cos\theta = 5\frac{m}{s}, \text{ therefore } u = \frac{5}{\cos\theta}$$

Now, solve for θ:

$$1.6\ m = \frac{u^2(1-\cos^2\theta)}{2 \times 9.81\ m/s^2}$$

$$1.6\ m \times 2 \times 9.81\frac{m}{s^2} = \frac{25(1-\cos^2\theta)}{\cos^2\theta}$$

$$\cos^2\theta = 0.44$$

$$\theta = 48.25^o$$

At an angle of 48.25 degrees, u is

$$u\cos\theta = 5\ \frac{m}{s} = u\cos 48.25$$

$$u = 7.51\ \frac{m}{s}$$

With a velocity of 7.51 m/s, and at an angle of 48.25 degrees, range of jump is

$$R = \frac{u^2\sin 2\theta}{g} = \frac{\left(7.51\frac{m}{s}\right)^2 \times \sin(2 \times 48.25)}{9.81} = 5.71\ m$$

Optimal distance from fence is half range of jump

$$d = 0.5 \times R = 0.5 \times 5.71 = 2.86n$$

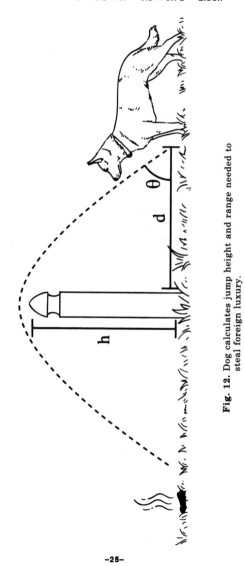

Fig. 12. Dog calculates jump height and range needed to steal foreign luxury.

ED-13. STEAL FOOD AT A BARBEQUE
PART I: THE GRILL

Advanced food stealing combines the human element, your growing background in physics, and a level of danger. Swiping a burger off the grill is a good a reason as any to advance your training. You know it takes 10s for your human to turn 150°, grab food, and return to the grill.

Begin your jump onto the chair within the right angle to jump but out of eyesight:

$$\tan\theta = \frac{height\ of\ human\ eyes - h_{chair}}{distance\ from\ human\ to\ right\ edge\ of\ chair} = \frac{1.7\ m - 0.5\ m}{2.75\ m}$$

$$\theta = 23.57^0$$

Then, calculate the distance needed to land on chair.

$$d = \tan\theta \times h_{chair} = \tan 23.57 \times 0.5\ m = 1.15\ m$$

Complete the jump in 1.7s to assure correct speed; ensure

$$horizontal\ displacement = d + (h_{chair} \times w_{chair}) = (u\cos\vartheta)\,t$$

$$1.15\ m + 0.5 \times 0.5m = (u\cos\vartheta) \times 1.7s$$

$$u\cos\theta = \frac{1.15m + 0.25m}{1.7s}$$

$$u = \frac{0.824\ \frac{m}{s}}{\cos\vartheta}$$

Using range formula, solve for ϑ

$$0.5\ m = \frac{u^2 \sin^2\vartheta}{2 \times 9.81\ \frac{m}{s^2}}$$

$$u^2(1 - \cos^2\vartheta) = 0.5\ m \times 2 \times 9.81\ \frac{m}{s^2}$$

$$\cos\vartheta = \sqrt{0.0647} = 0.2544$$

$$\vartheta = 75.26^0$$

Now, find the speed of jump.

$$u = \frac{0.824\ \frac{m}{s}}{\cos\theta} = \frac{0.824}{\cos 75.26} = 3.24\ \frac{m}{s}$$

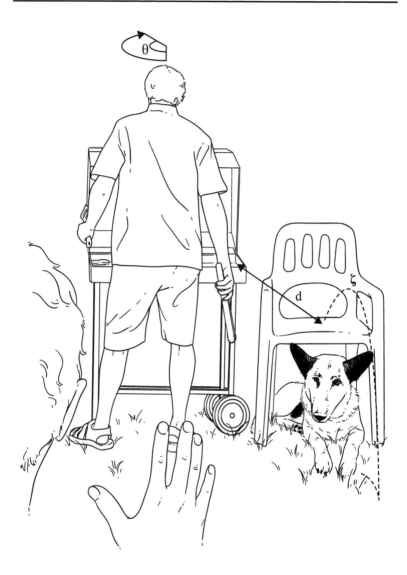

Fig. 13. Dog plots daring move to swipe burger off hot grill.

ED-14. STEAL FOOD AT A BARBEQUE
PART II: PLATES ON LAPS

Humans at BBQs tend to place their drinks on the ground, presenting a unique opportunity for food. To reach for this drink they must first turn their head, potentially putting their plate out of sight. Given,

θ_{los}: the human's line of sight $\approx 135°$

θ_d: the angle between the human's line of sight and its drink

You can calculate whether or not the human will still be able to see his food while grabbing his drink. First, the human only needs to turn by half its line of sight:

$$\theta_{turn} = \frac{\theta_{los}}{2} = 67.5°$$

If $\theta_d > \theta_{turn}$ then the food plate will be out of the human's sight for an angle of ($\theta_d - \theta_{turn}$)°. In this case, $\theta_d = 180°$.

Using this angle and approximating how fast a human turns gives us an equation for how long the food will be out of sight where,

t_{food}: time available to eat food,

ω: degrees per second of human's turn $\approx 80°$

t_{drink}: human's pause time while grabbing drink $= 0.5s$

$$t_{food} = \frac{(\theta_d - \theta_{turn})}{\omega} + t_{drink}$$

$$t_{food} = \frac{(180 - 67.5°)}{80} + 0.5s = 1.90s$$

Trends of note:

As angle θ_d increases, t_{food} increases.

As ω increases, t_{food} decreases.

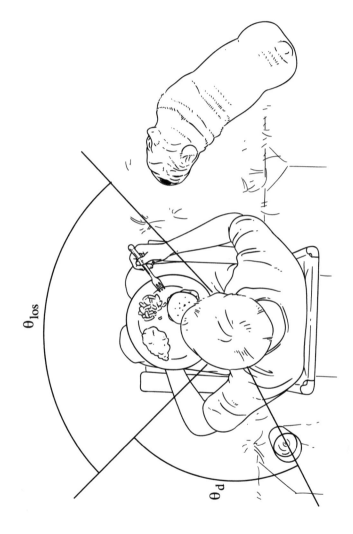

Fig. 14. Dog uses knowledge of human habit to plan food theft.

ED-15. STEAL FOOD AT A BARBEQUE
PART III: FOOD IN HANDS

Your third alternative to acquiring food at a barbeque is the most readily available, food in the hands of small humans. They put up the least resistance and are almost always covered in a cornucopia of tastes.

In order to grab the food first ensure the target is on the ground. Since they present no resistance, focus your attention on the proximity of the humans in the yard. To determine which target to pursue calculate the Vulnerability (V) of each, pursue the target with the highest Vulnerability.

$$V = \frac{\left(\begin{array}{c}\text{distance between} \\ \text{target and human}\end{array}\right)}{\left(\begin{array}{c}\text{distance between} \\ \text{target and dog}\end{array}\right)} + \left(\begin{array}{c}\text{number of handfuls} \\ \text{of food target is in} \\ \text{possession of}\end{array}\right) = \frac{d_b}{d_d} + n_{hf}$$

Three potential targets are in attendance. Compare the Vulnerability of each then determine the necessary speed to acquire the food.

Target 1	Target 2	Target 3
$d_b = 2\,m$	$d_b = 1.1\,m$	$d_b = 2.4\,m$
$d_d = 2.1\,m$	$d_d = 2.6\,m$	$d_d = 1.8\,m$
$n_{hf} = 1.2$	$n_{hf} = 2.1$	$n_{hf} = 0.94$
$V = \frac{2}{2.1} + 1.2 = 2.15$	$V = \frac{1.1}{2.6} + 2.1 = 2.52$	$V = \frac{2.4}{1.8} + 0.94 = 2.27$

Target 2 has the highest Vulnerability. Calculate the time it takes the human to reach the target, assume a 1s delay in reaction time for the human and a speed of 0.9 m/s. Then calculate the speed required to acquire the food before the human reaches the target.

$$t_b = \frac{d_b}{v_h} = \frac{1.1\,m}{0.9\,m/s} = 1.22\,s$$

$$v_d = \frac{d_d}{(t_b + 1)} = \frac{2.6\,m}{2.22\,s} = 1.17\frac{m}{s}$$

Fig. 15. Dog identifies proper target for brash grab-and-dash plot.

ED-16. EAT CAT FOOD

Your final food lesson is simple: you need to get to the cat food before the cat.

Calculate the time it takes for the cat to jump from the top of the cabinet

$$\Delta z = -2.13m \qquad\qquad\qquad v_{oz} = 0$$

$$a_z = -g = -9.81\frac{m}{s^2}$$

$$\Delta z = v_{oz}t + \frac{1}{2}a_z t^2$$

$$-2.13m = 0 + \frac{1}{2} \times 9.81\frac{m}{s^2}t^2$$

$$t = \sqrt{\frac{2.13m \times 2}{9.81\frac{m}{s^2}}} = 0.66s$$

Calculate the force required to propel yourself across the floor.

$$d = 3m \qquad\qquad\qquad \theta = 35°$$

$$\Delta x = d\cos\theta \qquad\qquad\qquad \Delta y = d\sin\theta$$

$$\Delta x = 3\cos 35 \qquad\qquad\qquad \Delta y = 3\sin 35$$

$$\Delta x = 2.46m \qquad\qquad\qquad \Delta y = 1.72m$$

$$v_{ox} = v_{oy} = 0$$

$$\Delta x = v_{ox}t + \frac{1}{2}a_x t^2 \qquad\qquad \Delta y = v_{oy}t + \frac{1}{2}a_y t^2$$

$$2.46m = 0 + \frac{1}{2}a_x(0.66s)^2 \qquad\qquad 1.72 = 0 + \frac{1}{2}a_y(0.66s)^2$$

$$\frac{2.46m \times 2}{0.66s^2} = a_x \qquad\qquad \frac{1.72 \times 2}{(0.66s)^2} = a_y$$

$$a_x = 11.29\frac{m}{s^2} \qquad\qquad a_y = 7.90\frac{m}{s^2}$$

Now, find the necessary force to propel yourself at that rate if you weigh 12kg.

$$F_x = 12kg \times 11.29\frac{m}{s^2} = 135.48N \qquad\qquad F_y = 12kg \times 7.90\frac{m}{s^2} = 94.8N$$

$$F = F_x \cos \theta + F_y \sin \theta$$

$$F = 135.48N \cos 35 + 94.8N \sin 35$$

$$F = 165.35N$$

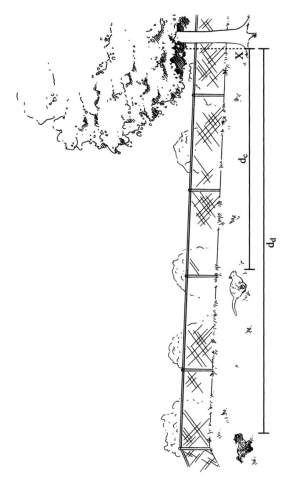

Fig. 16. Dog takes on archenemy in race to unguarded food.

LESSONS IN THIS CHAPTER

EXACT REVENGE, ESCAPE CERTAIN DEATH

Though the biological responses of fight and flight couldn't be more different, their success is assured when canine physics is applied to their tactics. Force and stealth play crucial roles in well-planned attacks and hasty retreats. Also of great importance in this chapter: Newton's Laws of Canine Motion.

RD-1. EAT A SHOE

The purpose and execution of this age-old habit are all for naught without the correct balance of variables in play. The enjoyment of eating the shoe (E) *must* outweigh the amount of emotional damage (ED) suffered by your human. Let *St* represent the shoe's tastiness, *I* stand for the Indulgence Factor, and t_o indicate the time owned.

$$E = \frac{StI}{t_o}$$

$$St = \frac{(\% \ leather) \times (Total\ time\ worn)}{(Number\ of\ times\ worn)} = \frac{I \times t_w}{t_n}$$

$$I = \frac{1000 \times (distance\ from\ comfy\ chewing\ spot)}{(Distance\ from\ shoe) \times (Laziness)} = \frac{1000 d_c}{d_s l_z}$$

Newton's First Law of Canine Motion comes into play in this situation. Having just woken up from a nap, your laziness factor is low. You spot mom's favorite shoes nearby. They aren't far from your favorite chewing spot. These shoes have the following values:

$$I = 85\%$$

$$t_w = 20 \ hrs$$

$$t_n = 8 \ times$$

$$l_z = 2$$

$$d_c = 10 d_s = 2 m t_o = 1440 hrs = 2 \ months$$

$$St = \frac{85 \times 20}{8} = 212.5$$

$$I = \frac{1000 \times 10}{2 \times 2} = 2500$$

$$E = \frac{212.5 \times 2500}{1440} = 368.9$$

E is positive: Newton's First Law of Canine Motion is in play. Now, calculate Emotional Damage.

$$ED = 10 \times (\# \ of \ shoes \ eaten)\left[shoe \ rank + 1000\frac{times \ worn}{time \ owned}\right] = 10S_e\left[r + 1000\frac{t_w}{t_o}\right]$$

$$S_e = 1 \qquad r = 12$$

$$ED = 10 \times 1\left(10 + \frac{1000 \times 20}{1440}\right) = 238.9$$

$$E = 368.9 > ED = 238.9$$

Your due diligence complete, you can enjoy your chew in peace.

Fig. 17. Dog uses as little energy as possible to enjoy best chew toy.

RD-2. EAT CLOTHES

Clothes are a soft, supple, tasty treat, but certain items are better than others. When choosing which items to grab from a clothesline, take the following into account.

s: the item's softness, a dimensionless coefficient

h: the height of the bottom of the item, in meters

h_{cl}: height of the clothesline, in meters

T: the item's tensile strength, in Pascals

T_{cl}: tensile strength of the clothesline, in Pascals

An item's Enjoyment curve, f(E), corresponds to the formula,

$$f(E) = s + \frac{Th}{T_{cl}h_{cl}} - \frac{h^2}{h_{cl}^2}$$

Analyzing this function we find many postulates regarding clothes:

Postulate 1: When $h/h_{cl} = 0$, nothing except the item of clothing's softness affects the Enjoyment curve.

Postulate 2: As h increases, an item's Enjoyment curve decreases exponentially.

Postulate 3: Though h causes the item's Enjoyment curve to decrease exponentially, it also causes Th to increase linearly. Therefore, higher items with greater tensile strength are preferable to those with low tensile strength.

Fig. 18. Dog postulates Enjoyment Curve held by unattended clean clothes.

RD-3. SHRED THE ROLL OF TOILET PAPER

When shredding a roll of toilet paper you want to maximize the spread of the mess, x_{mess}.

Assume all pieces of toilet paper ripped from the roll have equal mass and neglect any drag

forces. First calculate the angular velocity.

$$\omega = \frac{95°}{0.2s} = 8.29 \frac{rad}{s}$$

Use $l_{snout} = 0.2\ m$ to calculate v_0.

$$v_0 = \omega \times l_{snout} = 8.29 \times 0.2 = 1.66 \frac{m}{s}$$

$$v_{0x} = v_0 \cos \emptyset \qquad\qquad v_{0y} = v_0 \sin \emptyset$$

Find $\emptyset$ to maximize x_{mess}.

$$x_{mess} = v_{0x}t = v_0 t\ cos\emptyset$$

t also depends on $\emptyset$. Use the y-direction velocity equation to determine $t(\emptyset)$.

$$v_{fy} = v_{0y} - gt \qquad\qquad v_{fy} = 0$$

$$0 = v_0 \sin \emptyset - gt$$

$$t(\emptyset) = \frac{v_0 \sin \emptyset}{g}$$

Plug this into the equation for x_{mess}.

$$x_{mess} = \frac{v_0{}^2}{g} \cos \emptyset \sin \emptyset$$

To find $\emptyset$ to maximize x_{mess} take the derivative of x_{mess} and set it equal to zero.

$$\frac{dx_{mess}}{d\emptyset} = \frac{v_0{}^2}{g}(-\sin^2 \emptyset + \cos^2 \emptyset) = 0$$

$$\cos^2\emptyset - \sin^2\emptyset = \cos 2\ \emptyset$$

$$2\emptyset = 90°$$

$$\emptyset = 45°$$

Use this value to calculate $x_{mess,max}$.

$$x_{mess,max} = \frac{v_0{}^2}{g} \cos \emptyset \sin \emptyset = \frac{1.65^2}{9.81} \cos 45° \sin$$

Fig. 19. Dog calculates angular velocity's impact on maximizing mess.

RD-4. SPREAD TOILET PAPER AROUND THE HOUSE

When your humans leave home without you, you must show them that action is unacceptable.

One way to do this is to unravel the entire roll of toilet paper and then carry it to various parts of the house.

To unravel the roll, determine the maximum force you can apply to a sheet of toilet paper before it rips. From previous experience you know the Yield Strength of the TP.

$$\sigma_{TP} = 5000 \frac{kg}{m^2} = \frac{F}{A}$$

$$F = A \times \sigma_{TP} = 5000 \frac{kg}{m^2} \times 1.1 \times 10^{-4} m^2 = 0.55 \ N$$

Now determine the force required to unravel the roll. Here, μ represents static coefficient of friction.

$$m_{TP} = 80 \ g = 0.08 \ kg \ ; \ \mu = 0.22$$

$$F_f = \mu \ m_{TP} \ g = 0.22 \cdot 0.08 \ kg \ \cdot 9.81 \frac{m}{s^2} = 0.17 \ N$$

You must apply a pulling force between these two values in order to unravel the roll.

$$0.71 \ N < F_{pull} < 0.55 \ N$$

Once the roll is completely unraveled you can commence with spreading it around the house.

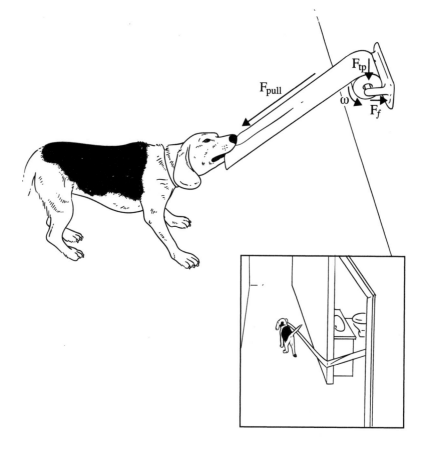

Fig. 20. Dog demonstrates frustration with nontraditional
TP tactics.

RD-5. PEE STRATEGICALLY INSIDE

It happens to every dog: the house is empty, the human won't be home for hours, and the dog needs to relieve itself somewhere. Rather than finding just any old corner in which to create a puddle, your pee can become the perfect, passive-aggressive reminder of your annoyance at your human. This kind of strategic peeing involves evaluating each potential peeing location with the formula for indoor relief revenge magnitude, which calculates the impact, less the effort.

$$r = visibility + smell\ retention + absorption\ rate - (distance)(laziness)$$

Every surface has its own smell, absorption, and visibility coefficients*:

	Visibility	Smell retention	Absorption
Wood	0.4781	0.1563	0.0638
Rug	0.2615	0.7825	0.5976
Tile	0.6917	0.0597	0.0396
Pillow	0.9281	0.3962	0.5615

Table 1. Coefficient table

*All values experimentally determined by the American Owner's Dog Association (AODA)

Assuming your laziness factor is 0.3 in this scenario, some common surfaces have the following revenge magnitudes:

$$r_{wood} = 0.4781 + 0.1563 + 0.0638 - (0.3)(0.15m) = 0.6532$$

$$r_{rug} = 0.2615 + 0.7825 + 0.5976 - (0.3)(1m) = 1.3416$$

$$r_{tile} = 0.6917 + 0.0597 + 0.0396 - (0.3)(1.5m) = 0.341$$

$$r_{pillow} = 0.9281 + 0.3962 + 0.5615 - (0.3)(3m) = 0.9858$$

Closer options become more desirable as laziness increases.

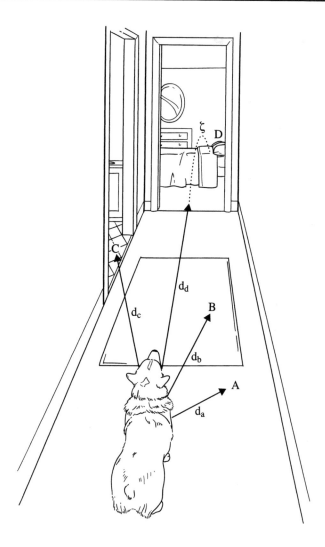

Fig. 21. Dog analyzes effect of voiding bladder on various convenient surfaces.

RD-6. POOP STRATEGICALLY INSIDE

When you are being blatantly ignored, revenge must be taken. To find the indoor excrement revenge magnitude (r_e), account for the poop's smelliness (Stinks units, S), the trouble it causes to your human (τ), the distance to location (d), the distance your human is to the location (d_h), your laziness factor (l), the warmth of the poop in degrees Celsius (w), and the horrified chill the appearance of the poop (a) will give your human (expressed in inverse degrees Celsius) :

$$r_e = \left(\frac{S\tau}{\ln\left(\frac{1+d}{1+d_h}\right)(l)} \right) \ln(wa)$$

Given standard bowel conditions of 35°C and 100kPa, poop can be assumed to have a smell rating of 8 Stinks units and warmth of 33°C. Poop usually ranks low on the horror scale; assume $a = 1$/°C except in extreme cases.

$$\ln(33 \times 1) = 3.50$$

For this lesson, solve for various locations. Assume your laziness factor is 1.

A: Wood floor behind human, a distance of 1 meter (d_h =1). Human notices nearly immediately and may step in pile (τ = 67%).

$$r_{eA} = \left| \frac{8\,S \times .67}{\ln\left(\frac{1+2\,m}{1+1\,m}\right)(1)} \right| 3.50 = 45.76\,S$$

B: Carpet in next room, a distance of 8 meters away from human. Human may not notice; carpet may need to be cleaned (τ = 34%)

$$r_{eB} = \left| \frac{8\,S \times 0.34}{\ln\left(\frac{1+6\,m}{1+8\,m}\right)(1)} \right| 3.50 = 37.88\,S$$

C: Throw rug in front of TV, a distance of 3 meters from human. Human cannot watch TV without cleaning poop; rug may need to be cleaned; human may step in poop if distracted by TV while walking (τ = 84%)

$$r_{eC} = \left| \frac{8S \times 0.84}{\ln{(\frac{1+4m}{1+3\,m})}(1)} \right| 3.50 = 105.40\,S$$

Location C scores the highest revenge magnitude, which happens to also have the largest trouble value but not the shortest distance for you. In this way, Newton's Laws remind us that the best revenge is taken when effort is balanced effectively with results.

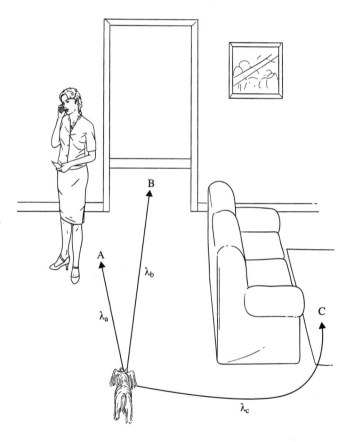

Fig. 22. Dog plans effective revenge-by-defecation.

RD-7. PUKE STRATEGICALLY INSIDE

Puking can easily be both a simple reaction to being sick and a statement to your human of his or her complicity in your nauseated state. Factors to consider in order to exact the highest revenge magnitude (r_p):

ρ: how concealed spot is, dimensionless

μ: how often human takes particular path, amount per day

K: risk of getting caught,

ε: distance of spot to current location

$$r = \frac{\rho^a \mu^b}{K^c \varepsilon^d}$$

This table shows values for three common puke targets as well as standard exponents for the equation. The exponents may be varied slightly depending on your specific revenge objectives.

	P	μ	K	ε
Target A	3	3	2	$d_a = 2$
Target B	2	1	1	$d_b = 3$
Target C	1	2	3	$d_c = 1$
Exponents	2	3	5	1

Table 2: Weighted table to exact revenge

Therefore, the standard equation for revenge when vomiting can be written as:

$$r = \frac{\rho^2 \mu^3}{K^5 \varepsilon^1}$$

Target A (depicted) has a revenge value of: $r_A = \frac{3^2 \times 3^3}{2^5 \times 2^1} = \frac{243}{64} = 3.79$,

while target C only has a revenge value of: $r_C = \frac{1^2 \times 2^3}{3^5 \times 1^1} = \frac{8}{243} = 0.03$.

For this scenario, to exact the best revenge with the least chance of getting caught, spot A should be chosen.

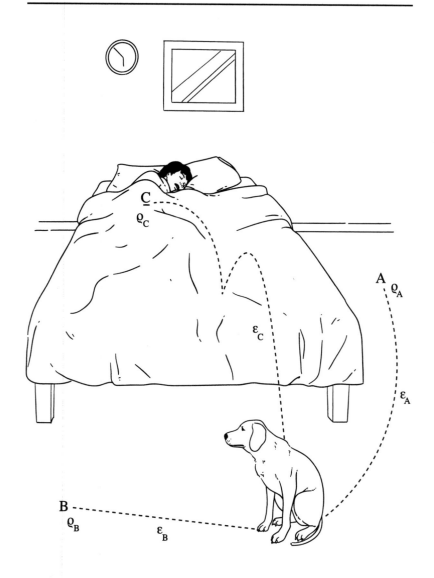

Fig. 23. Dog seeks effective method of notifying human of and relief from queasy feelings.

RD-8. BRING DOWN YOUR ENEMIES
PART I: THE MAILMAN

This classic situation hardly needs an introduction. The mailman stakes out your lawn six days a week, removes paper *your* human put there *purposefully*, and replaces it with paper that usually makes your human grumble. To take care of this predictable nemesis, wait behind a bush and calculate a fail-proof attack.

Here, the mailman's walking speed is 2.22 *m/s* and has 13.5*m* to the mailbox. Using the formula for speed, you can determine that t_{human} = 6.08s

Now determine the acceleration (a_{dog}) you must reach to cross the distance from your hide-out to the mailbox in the given time. Assume the following values for variables:

d_{dog}: distance of dog from mailbox = 18.75*m*

u_{dog}: initial speed of dog = 0 *m/s*

t_{dog}: time dog has to run to mailbox to intercept mailman (is equal to t_{human}) = 6.08s

$$d_{dog} = u_{dog}t_{dog} + \frac{1}{2}a_{dog}(t_{dog})^2$$

$$18.75 \; m = 0 + 0.5(a_{dog})(6.08)^2 \; s^2$$

$$a_{dog} = \frac{2 \times 18.75 \; m}{6.08^2 \; s^2} = 1.014 \; \frac{m}{s^2}$$

Finally, find the final velocity (v_{dog}) you must maintain to intercept the mailman at the mailbox:

$$(s_{dog})^2 = (u_{dog})^2 + 2a_{dog}d_{dog} = 0 + 2 \times 1.014\frac{m}{s^2} \times 18.75 \; m = 38.02\frac{m^2}{s^2}$$

$$s_{dog} = \sqrt{38.02\frac{m^2}{s^2}} = 6.17 \; \frac{m}{s}$$

Fig. 24. Dog plots classic attack on breed nemesis.

RD-9. BRING DOWN YOUR ENEMIES
PART II: THE VACUUM

There is no greater coward than a vacuum. It charges and retreats with no regard to your displays of aggression, submission, or curiosity. For your own safety, you must simultaneously attack with fervor and defend your position with care.

The enemy vacuum's potential area of attack forms a circle around its center described by,

$$(x - a)^2 + (y - b)^2 = r^2$$

where, (a,b) and (x,y) are the coordinates of the vacuum and the radius of the vacuum's potential attack (r) is approximately 1.2m. The vacuum may also move in any direction with a speed of 0.7m/s, shifting its Area of Effect (AoE) at the same rate.

Assume the vacuum is located at (0, 0). Keep a sufficient perimeter so that any direction the vacuum moves, you will not be encompassed by its AoE after one second of motion. Find the circle describing this sufficient perimeter.

$(a, b) = (0, 0)$ (Perimeter is centered at vacuum's current location)

$r = 1.2m + 0.7m = 1.9m$ (Radius is attack radius plus movement potential)

$x^2 + y^2 = 3.61$ (Equation of perimeter's bounds)

Risks can be taken by barking closer than this circle allows but extreme care must be taken in the event the vacuum moves back in your direction! If your reaction time is 0.25 seconds. Then,

$0.7 \, ^m/_s \times 0.25s = 0.175m$ (Distance vacuum can move in reaction time)

$r = 1.2m + 0.175m = 1.375m$ (New radius based on new distance travelable)

$x^2 + y^2 = 1.89m$ (New, riskier perimeter equation)

Though using this second equation allows you to attack closer, compensate for the time you may spend dodging the vacuum's movement, and the risk you take of it attacking you. Use caution!

Fig. 25. Dog takes on fickle attack-and-retreat patterns of roaring foe.

RD-10. BRING DOWN YOUR ENEMIES
PART III: THE MIRROR DOG

The mirror dog is a tricky foe. No matter what trick you pull, the mirror dog always seems to have a counter to match your speed and cunning. Your only hope of success is catching the mirror dog when its view of you—and your view of it—is blocked.

This box is 0.4m high. Your plan of attack should be to land on the middle of the box, 0.2m from the edge, to surprise and defeat the mirror dog. You know that the mirror dog can see anything standing 0.5m above the box. Find the angle within which the mirror dog can't see you:

$$\tan \theta = \frac{height\ of\ mirror\ dog}{length\ of\ box} = \frac{0.5\ m}{0.4\ m} = 1.25$$

$$\theta = \tan^{-1}(1.25) = 51.34^o$$

Then find out the maximum distance (d_{max}) from the box within which you can hide:

$$d_{max} = \frac{height\ of\ box}{\tan \theta} = \frac{0.4\ m}{\tan 51.34} = 0.32\ m$$

Hiding at 0.32m from the box creates a total horizontal distance (d_h) of 0.52m to jump during your attack. For safety, increase the height of your jump (h_{max}) to 0.1m above the height of the box. Land the jump within 0.75 seconds so that the mirror dog doesn't have time to react. Begin solving for the angle at which you should jump (θ):

$$u \cos \theta = \frac{d_h}{t} = \frac{0.52m}{0.75s}$$

$$u \cos \theta = 0.693\ \frac{m}{s}$$

$$\cos \theta = \frac{0.693\frac{m}{s}}{u}$$

Once you know the value of $\cos\theta$, you can begin solving for the jump's velocity (u):

$$u^2 (\sin \theta)^2 = h_{max}2g = 0.5\ m \times 2 \times 9.81 \frac{m}{s^2}$$

$$9.81\ \frac{m^2}{s^2} = u^2(1 - \cos^2 \theta) = u^2 \left(1 - \frac{0.693^2}{u^2}\right)$$

$$u = \sqrt{9.81 + 0.481} = 3.21 \ m/s$$

Now return to the first problem and solve for θ:

$$\cos \theta = \frac{0.693 \frac{m}{s}}{u} = \frac{0.693 \frac{m}{s}}{3.21 \frac{m}{s}}$$

$$\theta = 77.5^o$$

To make jump, you must leap with a velocity of 3.21 *m/s* at a 77.5° angle to the horizontal.

Fig. 26. Dog plans surprise strategy to best odd and annoy-ing rival.

RD-11. BRING DOWN YOUR ENEMIES
PART IV: THE TV DOG

The TV dog is unlike any other dog you may come across.

$$x \times y \times z = volume$$

$$.3m \times .7m * 0m = 0m^3$$

$$.4m \times .5m * 0m = 0m^3$$

No matter how big it looks

its volume is always

zero

No matter where you see TV dog, its bark comes from somewhere else.

No matter how loudly you bark, it never responds.

The volume of TV dog's bark changes widely without any noticeable effort.

TV dogs perform strange actions such as: playing basketball, drive cars, speak with humans.

No attacks from TV dog have been reported as of this writing.

Given,

> d: horizontal distance from TV dog
>
> θ: angle to TV dog from horizontal l= 28°
>
> d: total distance away from TV dog = 0.57m

$$d = d/\cos\theta$$

$$d = 0.57m / \cos(28°) = .64m$$

In order to stay safe,

If TV dog is barking, ensure d > 0.8m

If TV dog is quiet, d > 0.5m is good enough

Do not venture closer than 0.18m, even if TV dog is sleeping.

Fig. 27. Dog safely, cautiously defends household against unpredictable adversary.

RD-12. GET OUT OF THE BATH

Getting out of the bath requires a bit of finesse. The soap and water decreases the friction between your paws and the tub surface, greatly increasing the risk of slipping. Determine the maximum force you can apply without slipping. Assume the coefficient of sliding friction with soap and water in the tub becomes 0.13.

$$F_s = \mu\, m_d\, g = 0.13 \times 16.1\ kg \times 9.81 \frac{m}{s^2} = 20.53\ N$$

This is the maximum x-direction force you can apply. Now determine the maximum angle you can use to jump out of the tub without slipping assuming you can apply an overall force of 1.5 times your mass-force.

$$F = 1.5\, m_d\, g = 1.5 \times 16.1\ kg \times 9.81 \frac{m}{s^2} = 157.94\ N$$

$$F_x = F \cos\theta \le 20.53$$

$$\cos\theta \le \frac{20.53}{157.94} \quad \therefore \quad 172.53° \ge \theta \ge 82.53°$$

Pushing at an angle of at least 82.53° you can use your full strength to get out of the tub without slipping.

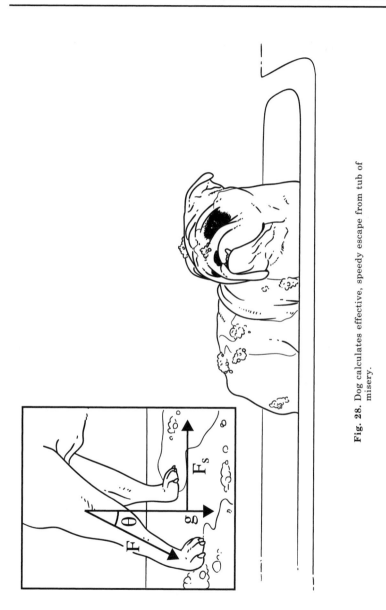

Fig. 28. Dog calculates effective, speedy escape from tub of misery.

RD-13. SLIP OUT OF YOUR COLLAR

It looks like magic when other dogs manage it: gracefully twisting out of a collar mystifies the

canine masses who think that simple pulling and tugging will do the trick. Behind the smoke and

mirrors is a time-tested formula sure to both save you in a pinch and frustrate a determined

human—or both!

Assume forces only in the x,y-plane:

F_h: your human's force

θ: angle of human's force relative to the ground

F_x: the x component of your human's force

F_y: the y component of your human's force

F_d: your required force

If your human pulls at a 45° angle from the ground with a magnitude of 250N then,

$$F_x = F_h \cos \theta$$

$$F_x = 250N \cos 50°$$

$$F_x = 160.69N$$

$$F_y = F_h \sin \theta$$

$$F_y = 250N \sin 45°$$

$$F_y = 191.51N$$

Now, dip your snout to angle of 45° (θ) and relax your ears. As humans typically only tighten

your collar to the circumference of your neck plus 2*in*, this move—if performed quickly

enough—will allow your human to pull the collar right off you if the combined force

components are greater than 300*N*. And in this case, it works!

You, of course, should be nowhere in sight by the time your human turns around.

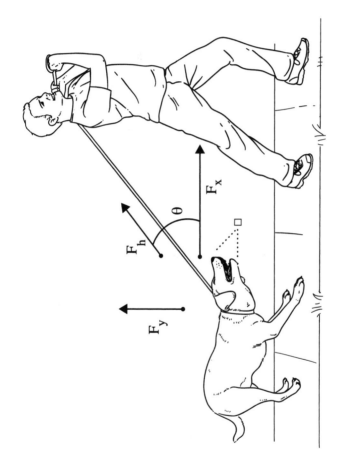

Fig. 29. Dog learns timeless escape technique.

RD-14. AVOID GETTING YOUR TEETH BRUSHED

You love your humans, but when they approach you armed with a toothbrush, you know that only bad things are to come. You must find a safe place to hide immediately.

Quickly calculating line of sight and factoring in variables that will work to your advantage is key. For example, you can hide under the bed, but many humans can still reach under and drag you out by your collar (if you chose this route by mistake, see RD-12. Slip out of your collar); however, a human with back problems may be at a loss.

Calculate how far under the bed you have to be for your human not to see you. Given the distance of your human to the bed (d_{hb} = 3m), your human's height (h_h = 1.6m), and the height of the space under the bed (h_{ub} = 0.5m), calculate the angle you must create to be successful (θ).

$$\tan \theta = \frac{1.1m}{3m}$$

$$\theta = 20.1363°$$

Next, calculate the angular distance between your human and the top of the bed (C_1), your human and you (C), and then the top of the bed and you (C_2).

$$C_1 = 3m^2 + 1.1m^2 = 3.1953m$$

$$\sin \theta = \frac{1.6m}{C}$$

$$C = \frac{1.6m}{\sin 20.1363°} = 4.6477m$$

$$C = C_1 + C_2$$

$$4.6477m = 3.1953m + C_2$$

$$C_2 = 1.4524m$$

Finally, find the distance under the bed to which you can safely retreat (d_{hide}).

$$\cos \theta = \frac{d_{hide}}{C_2}$$

$$d_{hide} = C_2 \times \cos \theta = 1.4524 \times \cos 20.1363° = 1.3636m$$

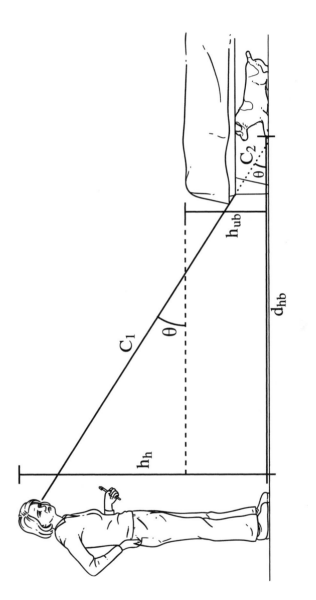

Fig. 30. Dog uses human's weakness to flee torture.

RD-15. AVOID GETTING YOUR NAILS CLIPPED

If you create a large enough mess then the nail clipping will get postponed. Calculate the

Impulse (I) needed to send the whole table crashing to the floor when you bump it at point x.

Find the initial velocity that sends the table crashing to the floor at 1.5 m/s. You also need to get

away from the scene at a speed of at least 2.0 m/s.

$$m_d = 11\ kg$$

$$v_{df} = 2.0\ \frac{m}{s}$$

$$m_t = 6\ kg$$

$$v_{ti} = 0\ \frac{m}{s};\ v_{tf} = 1.5\ \frac{m}{s}$$

$$I_t = I_d = \Delta p_t = p_f - p_i = m_t(v_{tf} - v_{ti}) = 6kg\left(1.5\frac{m}{s} - 0\frac{m}{s}\right) = 9\ \frac{kgm}{s}$$

$$9\frac{kgm}{s} = m_d(v_{df} - v_{di}) = 11kg\left(2.0\frac{m}{s} - v_{di}\right)$$

$$0.82\frac{m}{s} = 2\frac{m}{s} - v_{di}$$

$$v_{di} = -1.18\ \frac{m}{s}$$

So you must run in the negative x direction at a speed of 1.18 m/s to create a large enough mess

to postpone the nail clipping.

Fig. 31. Dog plans diversionary "accidents" to delay unnec-
essary grooming.

RD-16. AVOID EATING PILLS

Spit all pills with enough force to send them far underneath a kitchen cabinet. Assume the pill's aerodynamics negate drag and that the pill's initial coordinates are (0,0).

$$m_{pill} = 3.24 \times 10^{-4} kg$$

$$\theta = 55°$$

$$y_{dog} = 0.3m$$

$$x_{dog} = 0.46m$$

$$F_{spit} = 4 \times 10^{-3} N$$

$$F_{yuck} = 1 \times 10^{-3} N$$

Solve for the velocity at which you can spit the pill.

$$F^1{}_i = F_{spit} F_{yuck} F_{grav} = F_{spit} F_{yuck} (m_{pill} g)$$

$$F^1{}_i = 4 \times 10^{-3} N \times 1 \times 10^{-3} N \times 3.19 \times 10^{-4} kg = 8.19 \times 10^{-3} N$$

$$F^1{}_{i,x} = F^1{}_i \sin \theta = (8.19 \times 10^{-3} N) \sin 55° = 6.71 \times 10^{-3} N$$

$$F^1{}_{i,y} = F^1{}_i \cos \theta = (8.19 \times 10^{-3} N) \cos 55° = 4.70 \times 10^{-3} N$$

$$a^1{}_x = \frac{F'_{i,x}}{m_{pill}} = \frac{6.71 \times 10^{-3} N}{3.24 \times 10^{-4} kg} = 20.65 \frac{m}{s^2} \qquad x^1 = y_{dog} \tan \theta = 0.3 \tan 55 = 0.43m$$

$$V^1{}_0 = 0$$

$$a^1{}_y = \frac{F'_{i,y}}{m_{pill}} = \frac{4.70 \times 10^{-3} N}{3.24 \times 10^{-4} kg} = 14.46 \frac{m}{s^2}$$

$$V^1{}_{f,x} = \sqrt{V_{f,0}{}^2 + 2 d_x \dot{x}} = \sqrt{0 + 2 \times 20.65 \frac{m}{s^2} \times 0.43m} = 4.21 \frac{m}{s}$$

Find the velocity at which you need to spit the pill.

$$V'_{f,x} = V_{i,x}{}^2$$

$$\Delta x = x_{dog} - \acute{x} = 1m - 0.43m = 0.57m$$

$$a_x{}^2 = \frac{-F_{fric}}{m_{pill}} = \frac{\mu m_{pill} g}{m_{pill}} = 0.2 \times 9.81N = -1.96\frac{m}{s^2}$$

$$V^2{}_{fx} = \sqrt{V^2{}_{o,x}{}^2 + 2a_x{}^2\Delta x} = \sqrt{4.21^2 - 2 \times 1.96\frac{m}{s^2} \times 0.57m} = 3.94\frac{m}{s}$$

$$V^1{}_{f,x} = 4.21\frac{m}{s} > V^2{}_{fx} = 3.94\frac{m}{s}$$

You can rest assured that your efforts to dispose of the pill will be successful.

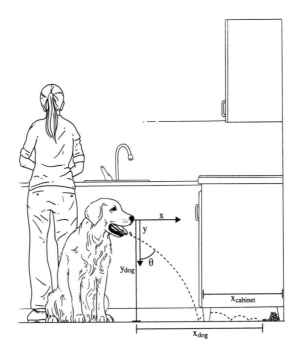

Fig. 32. Dog devises long-term solution to foil human's attempts to administer medication.

LESSONS IN THIS CHAPTER

WHEN
OUTSIDE

Dogs are often at their best outdoors, and those mastering canine physics are no exception. With the right calculations, your neighborhood can turn into a sanctuary of gratifying games and long-awaited successes. Speed, velocity, and projectile motion are essential tenets of this chapter's lessons.

O-1. CATCH CATS

You've tried to catch the neighbor's cat a hundred times before, but it's likely that you've never actually planned ahead to calculate your success. The speed needed to catch a cat before it reaches a tree can be described as,

$$s_d = \frac{d_d}{d_c/s_c}$$

where, s_d is your required speed, d_d is your distance from the tree (8m), d_c is the distance from the cat to the tree (5m), and s_c is speed of the cat (6m/s).

$$s_d = \frac{8\,m}{5\,m/6\,m/s}$$

$$s_d = \frac{8\,m}{.83\,s}$$

$$s_d = 9.64\,m/s$$

Estimate cat speeds as follows:

If cat is large, $s_c = 5\ m/s$.

If cat is medium, $s_c = 6\ m/s$.

If cat is small, $s_c = 7\ m/s$.

If cat is fluffy, subtract 1 m/s from drag.

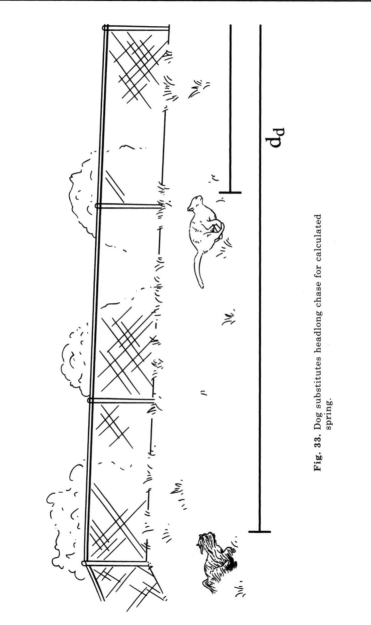

Fig. 33. Dog substitutes headlong chase for calculated spring.

O-2. CATCH SQUIRRELS

Though you want to catch them as much as you do cats, squirrels are likely to leave you barking at air. Before you dart after them, make sure you *can* catch them and make adjustments to your reaction based on your previous experiences with squirrels.

$$V_s = 5.36 \frac{m}{s}$$

$$d_s = 6m$$

$$d_d = 8m$$

$$t = \frac{d_s}{V_s} = \frac{6m}{5.36 \frac{m}{s}} = 1.12s$$

$$V_d = \frac{d_d}{t} = \frac{8m}{1.12s} = 7.14 \frac{m}{s}$$

Your max speed is 10*m/s* so you know you can catch the squirrel.

In order to decide if you will chase the squirrel, though, you must calculate the OhMyGod value when you catch it.

$$OhMyGod = \frac{1 + \# \; animals \; previously \; chased}{1 + \# \; of \; animals \; previously \; caught} \times \frac{volume \; of \; animal}{volume \; of \; dog}$$

$$v_{squirrel} = 20cm * \pi(2cm)^2 = 251.33cm^3$$

$$v_{dog} = 60 \times \pi(10cm)^2 = 18,849.56cm^3$$

$$OhMyGod = \frac{1361}{2} \times \frac{251.33cm^3}{18,849.56cm^3} = 9.07$$

Compare your result to the OMG reaction table to determine what you should do.

OMG factor	Reaction
OMG < 1	Chase after that thing like your life depends on it
1.01 ≤ OMG < 5	Chase with a good effort
5.01 ≤ OMG <10	Make it look like you really want to get it
10.01 ≤ OMG < 15	Advance half-way and bark ferociously
15.01 ≤ OMG <20	Stand and bark from where you are
20.01 ≤ OMG	Run away

Table 3. OMG Factors and Appropriate Reactions

Fig. 34. Dog analyzes facilities to catch arboreal rodent and effect of excitement on such ability.

O-3. PEE STRATEGICALLY OUTSIDE

When walking with your human, wait for the most opportune moment to pee to first maximize

the length of your walk, but secondly to increase your human's Emotional Damage factor (and,

subsequently, your Enjoyment factor) for your walk.

Determine the work (W) necessary to wait until your human stops to talk to a friend with a

smaller human in the rolling chair-like contraption. The force (F) required to lift your leg is 10N.

The height of your leg (Δy) is 0.37m. The force required to hold your pee (H) is 12.5N. The

distance (Δx) over which you must hold your pee is 1.2m. (Note: This equation is true, if and only

if the forces are spatially invariant.)

$$W = F\Delta y + H\Delta x = 10N \times 0.37m + 12.5N \times 1.2m = 18.7Nm$$

Compare the work required to your human's Emotional Damage factor. If W < E, then waiting is

worth the effort. Assume the following values for your human's condition:

$$P = \text{\# of poeple likely to see dog} = 4$$

$$F_s = \text{force required to stop dog} = m_d g = 13.2 \times 9.81 = 129.492N$$

$$d_{home} = \text{distance from home} = 1m$$

$$d_{person} = \text{distance from nearest person} = 0.6m$$

$$d_{dog} = \text{distance from dog} = 0.4m$$

$$ED = PF_s\left(\frac{d_{home}}{d_{person}} + d_{dog}\right) = 4 \times 129.492N \times \left(\frac{1m}{0.6m} + 0.4m\right) = 8{,}839.99Nm$$

$$W = 18.7Nm \ < ED = 8{,}839.99Nm$$

You can conclude that this strategic pee will be worth the wait.

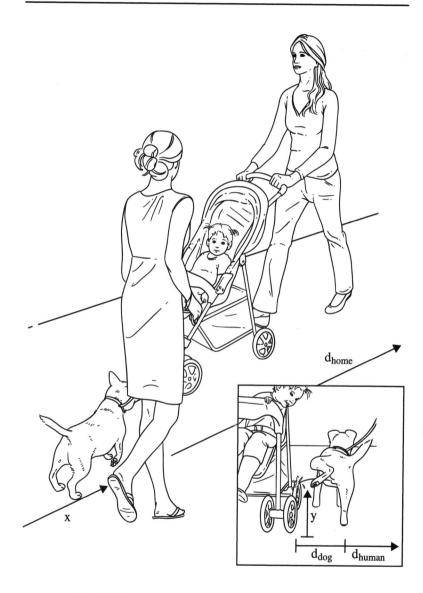

Fig. 35. Dog turns normal walk into a worthwhile memory.

O-4. POOP STRATEGICALLY OUTSIDE

Just because you're pooping where you're supposed to doesn't mean you can't improve your

tactics. Poop, after all, is a way to mark your territory and a clean yard is an unclaimed yard.

Choose a spot to poop that Is just out of sight of your human. Determine the best spot by

calculating its Find Value (FV, expressed in units of $^1/_m$) based on its findability (γ) and its

distance from the house (d_h)

$$FV = \frac{\gamma}{d_h}$$

For values of γ, use a field-tested table from a reliable source. The following table is based on

the formulas and theorems of excrementologist Jorriah P. Stinks.

Location	γ	d_h	FV
a in middle of the yard	1000	20m	50 $^1/_m$
b on side of yard	100	25m	4 $^1/_m$
c under a tree	90	19m	4.74 $^1/_m$
d under a bush	60	15m	4 $^1/_m$
e under a thorny bush, next to a fence, at the back of the yard	1	22m	0.045 $^1/_m$

Table 4. Stinks's Find value

The lower the FV, the better the spot as your poop will be harder to find. Location e, in this

instance, is most effective. Your humans will smell it but will not be able to find it.

Fig. 36. Dog masters tactical defecation.

O-5. CHASE INSECTS
PART I: CREEPY CRAWLIES

There's something tantalizing about chasing tiny bugs. Though it's doubtful that you *couldn't*

catch them, physics can help you catch them more efficiently.

Wait until at least 3 bugs are within your line of sight. Judging the speed of each insect you can

calculate the time to strike.

$$v_1 = 0.41 \frac{m}{s}; d_1 = 0.20 \, m$$

$$v_2 = 0.12 \frac{m}{s}; d_2 = 0.35 \, m$$

$$v_3 = 0.30 \frac{m}{s}; d_3 = 0.13 \, m$$

$$v_4 = 0.15 \frac{m}{s}; d_4 = 0.07 \, m$$

You know $v = \frac{d}{t}$ so calculate t from $= \frac{d}{v}$.

$$t_1 = 0.49 \, s$$

$$t_2 = 2.92 \, s$$

$$t_3 = 0.43 \, s$$

$$t_4 = 0.47 \, s$$

With minimal side to side deviance you can catch 3 bugs with one strike, maximizing your strike

efficiency.

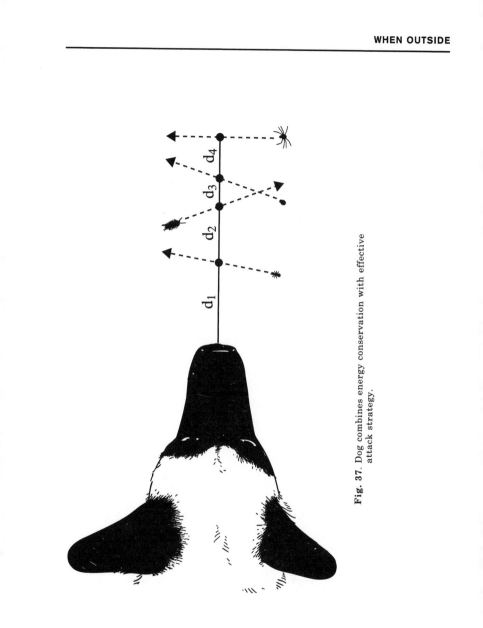

Fig. 37. Dog combines energy conservation with effective attack strategy.

O-6. CHASE INSECTS
PART II: FLYING INSECTS

Whether you're chasing butterflies for fun or snapping at pesky mosquitoes, it's good to know how to end the game when you really want to, and fill your stomach at the same time. This equation's variables will be,

s: length of snout =7cm

h: vertical distance from strike point

d_{dog}: full distance from strike point

d_{insect}: insect's distance from strike point

θ: angle from horizontal of insect's trajectory

v: insect's velocity relative to strike point = 1 m/s.

$$d_{dog} = \sqrt{7cm^2 + 20cm^2} = 21.189cm$$

The insect's distance from the strike point can be determined using,

$$\sin \theta = \frac{h/2}{d_{insect}}$$

$$d_{insect} = \frac{h}{2\sin \theta}$$

Given its velocity, determine how long it will take to reach the strike point.

$$t_{insect} = \frac{d_{insect}}{v} = \frac{d_{insect}}{1\frac{m}{s}} = d_{insect}$$

Assuming dog speed of 3m/s, dog will reach strike point in,

$$t_{dog} = \frac{d_{dog}}{3\frac{m}{s}} = 0.07063s$$

Now, leap to catch the flying insect in $t_{insect} - t_{dog}$ seconds

$$\frac{h}{2\sin \theta} - .07063s$$

and catch a tasty snack!

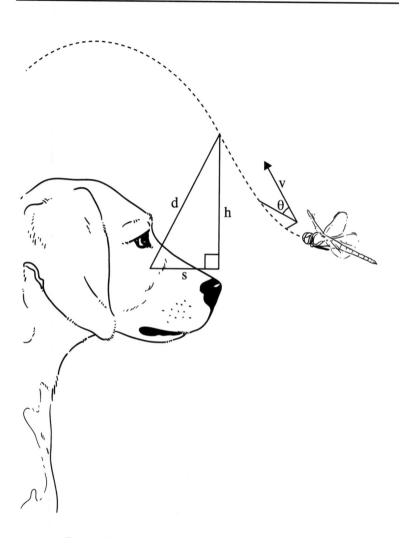

Fig. 38. Dog merges protein consumption with introductory mid-air interception.

O-7. CHASE BICYCLES

Chasing a bicycle is tricky. You have no true intention of *catching* the bicycle because, though the bike incites your uncontrollable rage, you know you'd never hurt the rider. You do, however, need to prepare yourself: getting too close could mean a firm kick in the snout by a trained athlete. These calculations should help.

The bicyclist's legs (L) are both 0.6m long. Should he kick backwards to shoo you away, his leg (L_B) will form an isosceles triangle (ABC) with his opposite leg (L_A). The angle (θ) of 50° formed by the intersection of AB will help you determine the distance his foot will travel (C).

The distance his foot will travel as he pedals can be determined by the Law of Cosines.

$$c^2 = 0.36m^2 + 0.36m^2 - 2(.6m)(.6m)\cos 50$$

$$c = \sqrt{.72m^2 - .36m^2} = 1m$$

You must, therefore, stay no less than 1m away from each forward-extended leg to stay out of kick range (d_{leg}). You must also consider that

$$d_{bark} \geq d_{leg}$$

or the rider may not hear you—making the chase truly pointless. Keeping the perfect distance requires maintaining appropriate speed (s_{dog}) compared to the bicycle (s_{bike}). Assume, then

$$s_{bike} = 6.7 \frac{m}{s}$$

$$s_{dog} = 8.05 \frac{m}{s}$$

Running at this speed will close the distance between you and the bicyclist's leg at a rate of 1.35m/s, so proper rate limiting measures must be taken.

These calculations are invalid for unicycles and tricycles.

Fig. 39. Dog practices cautious pursuit of a human-powered vehicle.

O-8. CHASE CARS

Though it was a more gratifying pastime when cars puttered along streets, chasing cars is still a time-honored canine tradition. It need not be disappointing with a touch of physics added; in fact, you may be able succeed in ways your predecessors only dreamed.

Calculate the force needed to chase this car uphill while your human chugs behind on a bicycle to which you are leashed. Assume you exert a constant force (F_{dog}) of 120N and that you are traveling up an incline (θ) of 15°.

$$W = F_{dog}\Delta d$$

$$\Delta x = 20m$$

$$\Delta y = \Delta x \tan \theta = 5.36m$$

$$\Delta d = \sqrt{\Delta x^2 + \Delta y^2} = 20.71m$$

$$W = 120N \times 20.71m = 2484J$$

Now calculate the likelihood of getting in trouble (L_t) for chasing the car. An L_t value above 20 guarantees that you will get in trouble.

$$L_t = \frac{W(\# \text{ times human yells to stop})}{1000} = \frac{2484J \times 15}{1000} = 37.26$$

Factor the amount of work you do into the amount of fun (F) you have (5.2 x 10⁵) to find the Force of Fun (F_{un}) in this situation.

$$F_{un} = \frac{F}{W} = \frac{5.2 \times 10^5 JN}{2484J} = 209.33N$$

The Force of Fun greatly outweighs the likelihood that you'll get in trouble. Therefore, it's worth charging after the car.

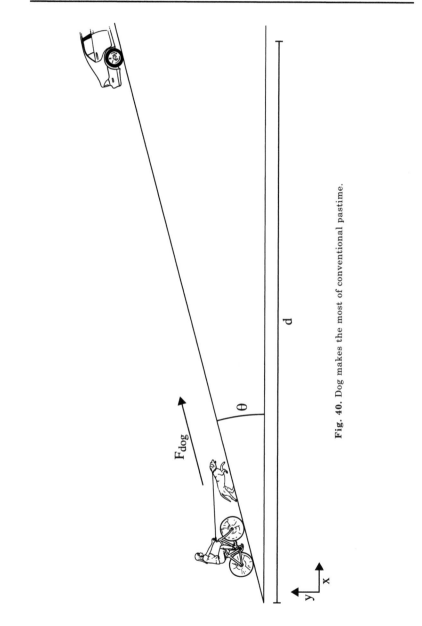

Fig. 40. Dog makes the most of conventional pastime.

O-9. CHASE SMALL CHILDREN

Children are fascinating pretend-prey. They have endless energy, and if you treat your attack as playful, you can earn just about any human's appreciation simply for being "cute." But just because children are practice targets doesn't mean there isn't an objective approach for winning your game.

Intercept the child at the angle shown ($\theta = 110°$) by calculating the time you need to wait before leaping forward.

The child has a mass of 25kg and is running with a speed of 2m/s. She is running in a perfect circle about the family car with a radius of 1.5m.

$$Arc\ length = \frac{\theta}{360} \times 2\pi r = \frac{110}{360} \times 2 \times \pi \times 1.5\ m = 2.88\ m$$

It will take her t_{kid} time to run the arc:

$$t_{kid} = \frac{arc\ length}{v_{kid}} = \frac{2.88\ m}{2\ \frac{m}{s}} = 1.44\ s$$

It will take you t_{leap} time to cross the 1.5m in a single bound:

$$t_{leap} = \frac{radius}{v_{dog}} = \frac{1.5\ m}{5\ \frac{m}{s}} = 0.3\ s$$

You should therefore wait t_{wait} time before leaping

$$t_{wait} = t_{kid} - t_{leap} = 1.44\ s - 0.3\ s = 1.14s$$

However, you should take care that leaping too fast could result in the child running into you.

Calculate the force of such an impact to reinforce your need to judge correctly

$$v_{kid} = radius \times angular\ velocity = r\omega$$

$$\omega = \frac{v_{kid}}{r} = \frac{2\ \frac{m}{s}}{1.5\ m} = 1.33\ \frac{rad}{s}$$

Also:

$$F_{kid} = ma$$

$$a = v_{kid}\omega$$

And so,

$$F_{kid} = mv_{kid}\omega = 25\,kg \times 2\frac{m}{s} \times 1.33\frac{rad}{s} = 66.5\,N$$

Though a 66.5N impact will be uncomfortable, you won't be injured. Just the same, remain

cautious, especially with larger children.

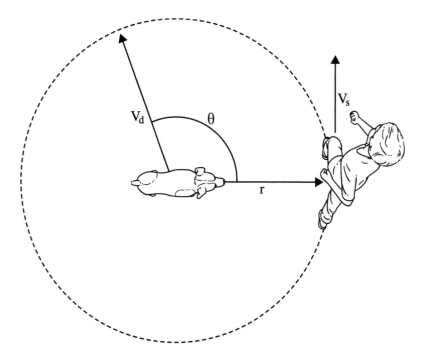

Fig. 41. Dog practices hunting techniques on small humans, albeit carefully.

O-10. WALK YOUR HUMAN

Your human may attempt to walk in the wrong direction or at the wrong pace. The solution is very simple. Apply an opposing force greater than your human's to set it back on the right track. Assume forces only in the x,y-plane:

F_h: your human's force

θ: angle of human's force relative to the ground

F_x: the x component of your human's force

F_y: the y component of your human's force

F_d: your required force

If your human pulls at a 38° angle from the ground with a magnitude of 250N then,

$$F_x = F_h \cos \theta$$

$$F_x = 250N \cos 38°$$

$$F_x = 197N$$

$$F_y = F_h \sin \theta$$

$$F_y = 250N \sin 38°$$

$$F_y = 153.92N$$

Since you are only trying to move forward, you must overcome F_x.

$$F_d > 197N$$

Overexerting yourself too far beyond this point could either pull your human over or exhaust you, neither of which are good ways to experience walking your human. Only exert forces greater than 250N through slow acceleration and never pull with a force greater than 300N.

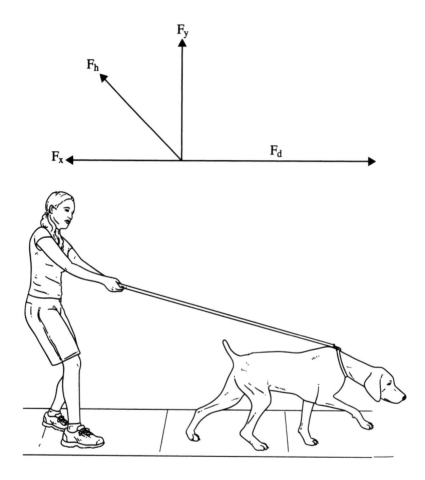

Fig. 42. Dog calculates force necessary to redirect human to proper path and pace.

O-11. WALK YOURSELF

When your human is overcome with laziness or is distracted, you must take things into your own paws and walk yourself.

Scoop up the leash in your mouth and embark. When your human sees you they will inevitably pursue at an increased rate. To continue to walk yourself you must maintain a distance greater than your human's reach. Calculate your human's reach (l_r) by taking note of her height (h_h)

$$h_h = 1.6\ m$$

$$l_r = 0.6\ h_h \cos \theta$$

Assuming the farthest your human can bend over and still walk gives you a minimum angle of 20° calculate your human's maximum reach.

$$l_{r,max} = 0.6\ h_h \cos \theta_{min} = 0.6 \times 1.6\ m \times \cos 20°$$

$$l_{r,max} = 0.902\ m$$

In order to continue to walk yourself you must stay at least 0.902 meters away from your human. Keep in mind that as your human's velocity increases the angle of reach increases as well. Therefore the faster pull you the smaller the distance you have to keep, but this is risky.

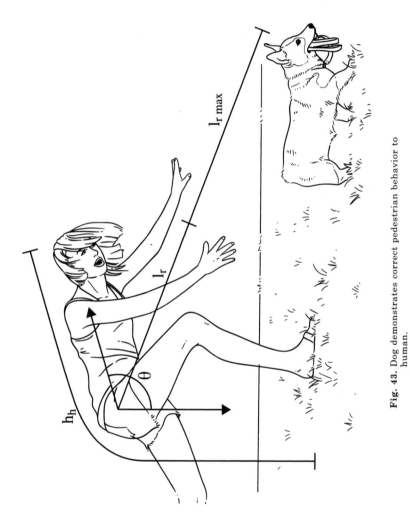

Fig. 43. Dog demonstrates correct pedestrian behavior to human.

O-12. RIDE IN A CAR
WITH THE WINDOWS DOWN

When riding with your head out of a window, you will experience sounds of unfamiliar

frequencies. To best account for what you hear, you can "translate" the frequencies based on

properties of the sounds you already know. Take, for example, another dog's bark from an

approaching car. Assuming the car is approaching directly towards you and given,

λ_1: frequency of the dog's bark $\approx$ 150 Hz,

v_s: velocity of the other dog $\approx$ 50 km/h,

v_r: your velocity $\approx$ 50 km/h,

v: velocity of sound waves through air $\approx$ 343

m/s,

λ_2: observed frequency of dog's bark,

then,

$$f = \left(\frac{v + v_r}{v + v_s}\right) f_0$$

However, since most cars will not approach directly, radial velocity must be used instead giving,

$$\bar{v}_r = v_r \times \cos\theta$$

$$\bar{v}_s = v_s \times \cos\theta$$

where,

$\bar{v}_r$: your radial velocity,

$\bar{v}_s$: other dog's radial velocity,

θ: angle between your forward motion and other dog.

Theta can be given as a function of time,

$$\theta = \tan^{-1}\left(\frac{(horizontal\ distance\ from\ dog)}{(forward\ distance\ from\ dog)}\right)$$

$$\theta = \tan^{-1}\left(\frac{1.2m}{2d - (v_r + v_s)t}\right)$$

Use the final formulas, to calculate how a dog's bark will sound from the moving car.

$$\theta = \tan^{-1}\left(\frac{1.2m}{7m - (v_r + v_s)t}\right)$$

$$\lambda_2 = \left(\frac{1234.8\ km/s + (v_r * \cos\theta)}{1234.8\ km/s + (v_s * \cos\theta)}\right)$$

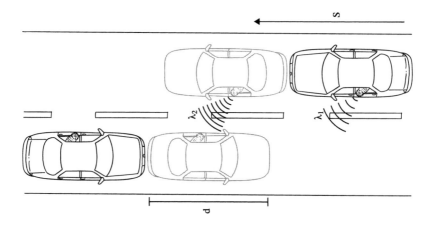

Fig. 44. Dog deciphers foreign sounds on a car ride.

O-13. PLAY FETCH FOR YOUR HUMAN

Fetching for your human is an ideal if not stereotypical scenario for canine physics. Use the range equation with which we've already worked to determine the max height of the ball (h_{max}). Air resistance is negligible. There is no force opposing horizontal motion

$$h_{max} = \frac{u^2(\sin\theta)^2}{2g} = \frac{(10\,\frac{m}{s})^2 \times (\sin 30)^2}{2 \times 9.81\,\frac{m}{s^2}} = 1.27\,m$$

t_1: time needed for ball to reach max height

$$t_1 = \frac{u\sin\theta}{g} = \frac{10 \times \sin 30}{9.81} = 0.51\,s$$

h_t : total height of ball relative to ground

$$h_t = height\ of\ person + h_{max} = 1.8\,m + 1.27\,m = 3.07\,m$$

t_2: time taken for ball to fall from max elevation to ground; u_1: velocity of ball at h_{max}

$$h_t = u_1 t_2 + 0.5g(t_2)^2$$

$$3.07\,m = 0 + 0.5 \times 9.81\frac{m}{s^2} \times (t_2)^2$$

$$t_2 = \sqrt{\frac{3.07\,m}{0.5 \times 9.81\,\frac{m}{s^2}}} = 0.79s$$

t_t: total time ball is in the air

$$t_t = t_1 + t_2 = 0.51\,s + 0.79\,s = 1.3\,s$$

x: distance ball covers horizontally

$$x = (u\cos\theta)t_t = (10\frac{m}{s} \times \cos 30)(1.3\,s) = 11.26\,m$$

After bounce, your instincts predict that the ball will travel one more meter in 0.5 s. Calculate the speed needed to catch the ball at this point.

$$dog\ speed = \frac{x + 1\,m}{t_t + 0.5\,s} = \frac{11.26\,m + 1\,m}{1.3\,s + 0.5\,s} = 6.81 m/s$$

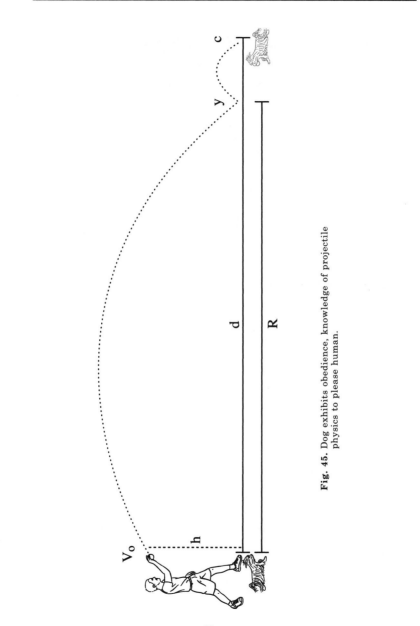

Fig. 45. Dog exhibits obedience, knowledge of projectile physics to please human.

O-14. PLAY FETCH WITH YOUR HUMAN

Fetching with your human is not dissimilar to fetching for your human, but you may need to take the time to train your human correctly. So you don't become impatient, you can track your human's progress with the following calculations. Remember, air resistance is negligible. There is no force opposing horizontal motion

$$h_{max} = \frac{u^2(\sin\theta)^2}{2g} = \frac{(10\,\frac{m}{s})^2 \times (\sin 30)^2}{2 \times 9.81\,\frac{m}{s^2}} = 1.27\,m$$

t_1: time needed for ball to reach max height

$$t_1 = \frac{u\sin\theta}{g} = \frac{10 \times \sin 30}{9.81} = 0.51\,s$$

h_t : total height of ball relative to ground

$$h_t = height\ of\ person + h_{max} = 1.8\,m + 1.27\,m = 3.07\,m$$

t_2: time taken for ball to fall from max elevation to ground; u_1: velocity of ball at h_{max}

$$h_t = u_1 t_2 + 0.5g(t_2)^2$$

$$t_2 = \sqrt{\frac{3.07\,m}{0.5 \times 9.81\,\frac{m}{s^2}}} = 0.79s$$

t_t: total time ball is in the air

$$t_t = t_1 + t_2 = 0.51\,s + 0.79\,s = 1.3\,s$$

x: distance ball covers horizontally

$$x = (u\cos\theta)t_t = (10\frac{m}{s} \times \cos 30)(1.3\,s) = 11.26\,m$$

Calculate the time (t_h) it will take your human to reach the ball and return. Assume your human's speed (s_h) is lessened to 1.34m/s by disappointment in your desire to change the game.

$$t_h = \frac{2x}{s_h} = \frac{2(11.26m)}{1.34\frac{m}{s}} = 16.8s$$

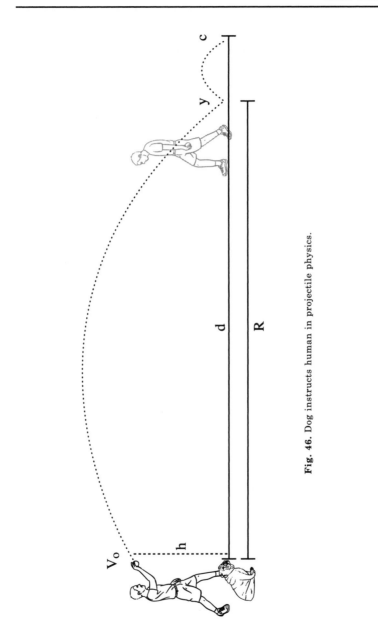

Fig. 46. Dog instructs human in projectile physics.

O-15. CATCH A FRISBEE

Catching a Frisbee is much like playing fetch but Frisbees fly differently than other toys. A successful Frisbee catch is done while the Frisbee is still in the air. You must first determine the trajectory of the Frisbee. The symbols (+) and (-) indicate upward and downward movement respectively. Assume the following for the Frisbee and calculate the initial forces. Note (+) and (-) denotations refer to positive and negative direction.

$$\theta_i = 10° \qquad v_i = 14\frac{m}{s} \qquad y_i = 1.0\ m \qquad \rho = 1.23\frac{kg}{m^3}$$

$$\omega_i = 10\frac{rad}{s} \qquad d_f = 0.2\ m \qquad m_f = 0.13\ kg$$

$$v_{ix} = v_i \cos\theta = 14\frac{m}{s} \times \cos 10° = 13.78\frac{m}{s} \qquad v_{iy} = v_i \sin\theta = 14\frac{m}{s} \times \sin 10° = 2.43\frac{m}{s}$$

$$C_D = 0.12 \qquad C_L = 0.24$$

$$F_D = \frac{1}{2}\rho\,v^2\,C_D = \frac{1}{2}\times 1.23\frac{kg}{m^3}\times 14^2\frac{m}{s}\times 0.12 = 14.64\ N$$

$$F_{Dx} = F_D \cos\theta = 14.64\ N \times \cos 10° = 14.41\ N\ (+)$$

$$F_{Dy} = F_D \sin\theta = 14.64\ N \times \sin 10° = 2.54\ N\ (-)$$

$$F_L = \frac{1}{2}\rho\,v^2\,C_L = \frac{1}{2}\times 1.23\frac{kg}{m^3}\times 14^2\frac{m}{s}\times 0.24 = 28.92\ N$$

$$F_{Lx} = F_L \sin\theta = 28.92\ N \times \sin 10° = 5.02\ N\ (-)$$

$$F_{Ly} = F_L \cos\theta = 28.92\ N \times \cos 10° = 28.48\ N\ (-)$$

$$F_{gy} = m_f\,g = 0.13\ kg \times 9.81\frac{m}{s^2} = 1.28\ N\ (-)$$

As the angular velocity of the Frisbee decreases by the drag force the Frisbee slows down and the lift force decreases.

$$F = ma \ \text{so:} \ F_x = m_f\frac{\Delta v_x}{\Delta t}\ ;\ F_y = m_f\frac{\Delta v_y}{\Delta t}$$

So to catch the Frisbee at exactly 0.5s from launch, you must match or beat the following velocities when you run:

$$\Delta v_x = \frac{F_x}{m_f}\Delta t = \frac{14.41\ N - 5.02\ N}{0.13\ kg} \times 0.5\ s = 36.11\ \frac{m}{s}$$

$$\Delta v_y = \frac{F_y}{m_f}\Delta t = \frac{-2.54\ N - 28.48 - 1.28\ N}{0.13\ kg} \times 0.5\ s = -124.23\ \frac{m}{s}$$

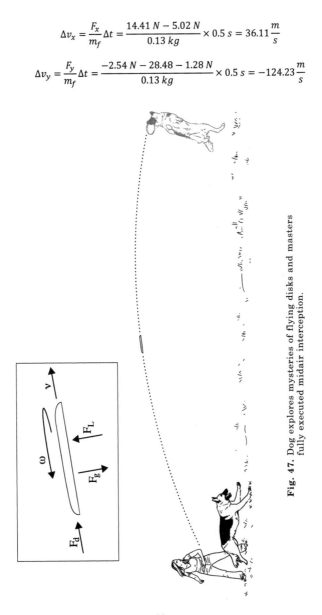

Fig. 47. Dog explores mysteries of flying disks and masters fully executed midair interception.

O-16. IDENTIFY THE BEST-SMELLING GRASS TO ROLL IN

Not all two grass patches are alike, and determining which patch is the best smelling no longer needs to be a lengthy process requiring multiple comparisons. Just calculate its Odor Magnitude (O) by assessing its ratio of dead thing (D_t) and poop content (P) to the content of fresh grass (G_f) it actually contains.

Example:

$$O = \frac{D_t + P}{G_f}$$

$D_{t1} = 5.28mg$

$P_1 = 11.12mg$

$G_{f1} = 129.87mg$

$$O = \frac{5.28mg + 11.12mg}{129.87mg} = 0.126$$

$D_{t2} = 6.04mg$

$P_2 = 9.82mg$

$G_{f2} = 131.69mg$

$$O = \frac{6.04mg + 9.82mg}{131.69mg} = 0.120$$

These two patches of grass may have taken you several minutes to accurately compare before, but this process makes your decision objective.

Your roll in the first grass patch should be completed according to the traditional canine standards: ensure θ > 100° and d > half the length of your back for the most effective coverage.

Fig. 48. Dog coats self with prime odors with least effort possible.

LESSONS IN THIS CHAPTER

JUST YOU AND YOUR HUMAN

As many of the lessons learned so far are perfected to send your human a negative message, work in contradiction to your human's wishes, and seek to cancel out the importance of their happiness for your own gratification, this chapter is devoted entirely to reclaiming and strengthening your relationship with your human while continuing to integrate new concepts and skills.

YH-1. WAKE UP YOUR HUMAN

You know your human hates the alarm clock, so take the initiative and wake your human up five minutes before it goes off. Determine the Force you must apply to the blankets to pull them off entirely. Assume your mass is 27.2kg. Your own needs play a large part in the calculation.

Need	Need Factor η
Water	1
Food	2
Pee	3
Play	4
Poop	5

Table 5. Need Factors, as defined by the UCLA of Barkley's Canine Psychology and Physiology department.

If you want to play, for example, you'd factor in η = 4.

$$F_N = \eta mg = 4 \times 27.2kg \times 9.81 \frac{m}{s^2} = 1067.33N$$

Compare this to the force necessary to overcome static friction (μ=0.62) and move the blankets ($m = 2kg$).

$$F_s = \mu_s F_N = 0.62 \times 2kg \times 9.81 \frac{m}{s^2} = 12.16N$$

You obviously have the strength necessary if your human does not offer up any resistance. Should your human attempt to keep the covers on the bed—and risk both sleeping in and not meeting your need—abandon this effort and jump onto the bed to lick your human's face. You are likely to startle sense back into your human.

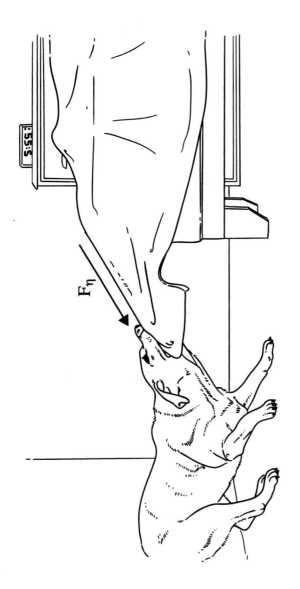

Fig. 49. Dog rouses human before alarm clock starts morning off wrong.

YH-2. GREET YOUR HUMAN AT THE DOOR

Sitting in your favorite but forbidden napping spot is a dangerous business. Save yourself the

trouble and determine the speed necessary to reach the door from the chair in 10s or less.

$$y_{chair} = 0.38m$$

$$t = 10s$$

$$x = 3.65m$$

$$d = \sqrt{x^2 + y^2} = 3.67m$$

$$V = \frac{d}{t} = \frac{3.67m}{10s} = 0.367\frac{m}{s}$$

When you reach the door, be sure to show your human how happy you are to see him or her so

your actions are seen as devoted and loving rather than suspicious (see YH-3. Greet your human

with a kiss).

Fig. 50. Dog calculates speed needed to prevent human from discovering daytime nap spot.

YH-3. GREET YOUR HUMAN WITH A KISS

Determine the work (w) required to jump up to lick your human's face. It requires 3 jumps to cover your human's whole face in slobber. First, calculate the time and speed of each jump to determine the acceleration and force and then the Work.

$$v_f^2 = v_0^2 + 2a\Delta y$$

$$v_f^2 = 0 + 2 \times 9.81 \frac{m}{s^2} \times 0.55m$$

$$v_f = 3.28 \frac{m}{s}$$

$$\Delta y = v_0 t + \frac{1}{2}at^2$$

$$0.55m = 0 + \frac{1}{2} \times 9.81 \cdot t^2$$

$$t^2 = \frac{2 \cdot 0.55m}{9.81 \frac{m}{s^2}} = 0.11 \; s^2$$

$$t = 0.33 \; s$$

$$a_{jump} = \frac{v}{t} = \frac{3.28}{0.33} = 9.94 \frac{m}{s^2}$$

$$F = m_{dog}a_{jump} = 31.75 \; kg \times 9.94 \frac{m}{s^2} = 315.6 \; N$$

$$w = 315.6 \times 0.55 = 173.58 \; J$$

$$w_{total} = 3 \times w = 3 \times 173.58 \; J = 520.74 \; J$$

(This assumes that when you jump, no kinetic energy is lost. Remember that kinetic energy loss is frowned upon in most canine physics communities as irresponsible.)

You, of course, know that showing your human affection excites you—especially if you human returned from any time spent out of your line of sight. Compare to the level of excitement you experience to determine if you will proceed.

$$Excitement \; Quotient = \frac{Time \; human \; was \; away}{Number \; of \; fun \; things \; chewed \; while \; alone}$$

$$Ex = \frac{t}{CN} = \frac{36000\,s}{5} = 7200\,s$$

Clearly the necessary work is outweighed by excitement.

Fig. 51. Dog compares excitement of reunion with human to work needed to cover face in slobber.

YH-4. KEEP YOUR HUMAN'S SEAT WARM

No human can deny the pull of a warm seat, and you can proactively show your human how much you care by ensuring that any seat they claim will be warm and ready for them upon their return.

To warm the seat most efficiently, calculate the largest area on which you can lay down.

If you occupy roughly these dimensions

$$h = 28cm$$

$$w = 30cm$$

$$d = 12cm$$

Your single largest coverage area will utilize the area created by your two longest dimensions; in this case it would be h X w—whether on your stomach or back.

$$A = 28cm \times 30cm = 840cm^2$$

Ensuring maximum warmth, however, is more the product of technique than of physics. For best results, jump into your human's seat as soon as they get up. If they are indecisive, feel free to nudge your human on his or her way as reassurance that you'll keep the spot perfectly cozy.

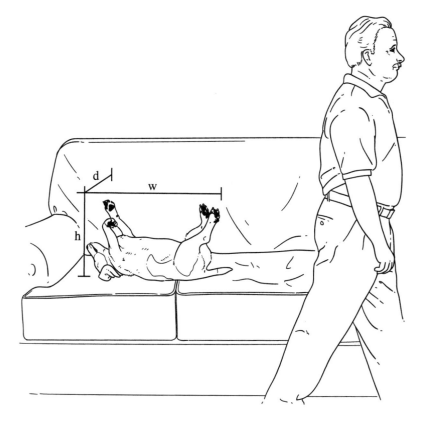

Fig. 52. Dog analyzes optimal heat loss prevention position.

YH-5. KEEP YOUR HUMAN'S BED WARM

In order to keep your human's bed warm you must use whatever means necessary to reach it.

Using the most readily available items create a path onto the bed. Determine the Work required

and compare that to the Elation Value to determine if this is the correct course of action.

Calculate Work and Elation Value for a Laundry Ramp. Assume laundry comes in discreet

masses.

Undies:

$$m_u = 0.23 \, kg$$

Pants:

$$m_p = 0.91 \, kg$$

Shirts:

$$m_s = 0.68 \, kg$$

$$\mu = 0.2 \text{ (cloth on}$$

wooden floor)

Determine the Force required to drag each item.

Undies: $F_u = (1 + \mu)m_u g = (1 + 0.2)0.23 \, kg \times 9.81\frac{m}{s^2} = 2.71 \, N$

Pants: $F_p = (1 + \mu)m_p g = (1 + 0.2)0.91 \, kg \times 9.81\frac{m}{s^2} = 10.71 \, N$

Shirts: $F_s = (1 + \mu)m_s g = (1 + 0.2)0.68 \, kg \times 9.81\frac{m}{s^2} = 8.00 \, N$

You will need 14 pieces of laundry; 5 Undies, 4 Pants, and 5 Shirts. All have to be moved a

distance of 1.35 m. Now calculate the total Work.

$$W = \left(5F_u + 4F_p + 5F_s\right)d$$

$$W = (5 \times 2.71 \, N + 4 \times 10.71 \, N + 5 \times 8.00 \, N) \times 1.35 \, m = 130.13 \, Nm$$

Compare this to the Elation Value, V_E, on the bed.

$$V_E = \left(\begin{matrix} comfiness\ of \\ celebration\ spot \end{matrix}\right) \times \left(\begin{matrix} Potential\ Energy \\ gained \end{matrix}\right) = C \times P = C\ m_d\ g\ h$$

Surface	Comfiness Factor
Cement	0.001
Dog bed	4.3
Human's bed	9.1
Human's pillow on bed	10.0

Surface	Comfiness Factor
Wood floor	2.6
Wood floor on hot day	7.6
Rug on wood floor	3.5
Couch	8.4

Table 6. Comfiness factor (C) for surfaces in question. Based on data gathered in the field by the authors.

$$V_E = 9.1 \times 10.2\ kg \times 9.81\ \frac{m}{s^2} \times 0.75\ m = 682.96\ Nm$$

Since $V_E \gg W$ the plan is good.

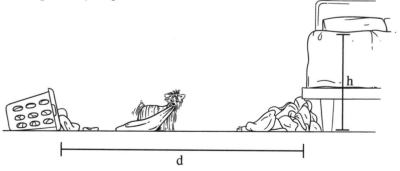

Fig. 53. Dog uses creative tactics to reach and warm tall bed.

YH-6. PASS THROUGH ALL DOORWAYS
BEFORE YOUR HUMAN

In order to accomplish this you have to quickly assess your human's speed. However, a good approximation is to use your human's average speed.

Point A	Point B	Distance (m)	Time (s)
Couch	Kitchen door	5	3
Couch	Front door	11	7
Kitchen table	Back door	4.6	4
Top of stairs	Bedroom door	9.2	7.6

Table 7. Time and Distance for this scenario.

$$v_{avg} = \frac{\frac{5}{3} + \frac{11}{7} + \frac{4.6}{4} + \frac{9.2}{7.6}}{4} = 1.4 \frac{m}{s}$$

Use this estimate to determine the necessary velocity you need to get through any door.

Calculate the necessary velocity given your human has approximately a $1s$ head start ($t_{hs} = 1\ s$) and you want to pass through all doors ahead of your human at a minimum distance of the length of your body ($l_d = 0.62\ m$).

$$t_h = \frac{d}{v_{avg}}$$

$$v_d = \frac{d + l_d}{t_h - t_{hs}}$$

Now calculate the necessary velocity for a trip from the couch to the front door.

$$t_h = \frac{d}{v_{ave}} = \frac{11\ m}{1.4 \frac{m}{s}} = 7.86\ s$$

$$v_d = \frac{d + l_d}{t_h + t_{hs}} = \frac{11\ m + 0.62\ m}{7.86\ s - 1\ s} = 1.69 \frac{m}{s}$$

Use this set of calculations to determine the velocity necessary to get through any given door.

Fig. 54. Dog asserts protective, loyal nature by racing through all doors first, no matter the initial position.

YH-7. EXIT ALL CARS BEFORE YOUR HUMAN

Your human hates being outside too long in the hottest and coldest weather, so it's important

you don't slow her down when exiting the car. The fastest way to get out of the car before your

human is to jump out from behind her when she leans forward to retrieve the car keys. This

gives you the opportunity to jump through the space created by the seat and human.

Calculate the momentum you have when you reach the door. You must have enough

momentum for your human to be unable to stop your exit when she grabs your leash.

$$P = mv$$

$$m = 20.41kg$$

In this small space, you can reach half of top speed.

$$V_{max} = 2.5\frac{m}{s}$$

$$V_{exit} = 1.25\frac{m}{s}$$

$$P = 20.41kg \times 1.25\frac{m}{s} = 225.51\frac{kgm}{s}$$

Now calculate the Force needed to stop you in $1s$.

$$F = \frac{dP}{dt} = \frac{25.51\frac{kgm}{s}}{1s} = 25.51N$$

Your human's normal pulling strength is equal to her weight.

$$m_h = 68.03kg$$

$$F_h = m_h g = 68.03kg \times 9.81\frac{m}{s^2} = 667.46N$$

So if she catches you all will be lost.

However, assuming you make it out of her reach in time, she will have to fumble to try to catch

the leash and you'll be away and free!

Fig. 55. Dog helps human increase travel efficiency by eliminating all delays in exiting vehicles.

YH-8. SIT ON YOUR HUMAN'S LAP

To sit on your human's lap, you must overcome the force exerted by your mass on the human.

To do this you must exert a Cuteness Force greater than your weight.

$$F_{cute} > F_{dog}$$

$$m_{dog} = 27.3kg$$

$$F_{dog} = 27.3kg \times 9.81\frac{m}{s^2} = 267.81N$$

The Cuteness Force is calculated as follows

$$F_{cute} = \frac{T_{dog}}{T_{room}} \times (angle\ \theta\ eyes\ make\ with\ face, in\ radians) \times 350N$$

$$T_{dog} = 102.5°F = 39.16°C = 312.15K$$

$$T_{room} = 70.16°F = 21.2°C = 294.2K$$

$$\theta = 76.8° = 1.34rad$$

$$F_{cute} = \frac{312.15K}{294.2K} \times 1.34 \times 350 = 492.6N$$

$$F_{cute} = 492.6N > F_{dog} = 267.81N$$

Your Cuteness Force *is* greater than your weight, so your human will let you cuddle on his lap.

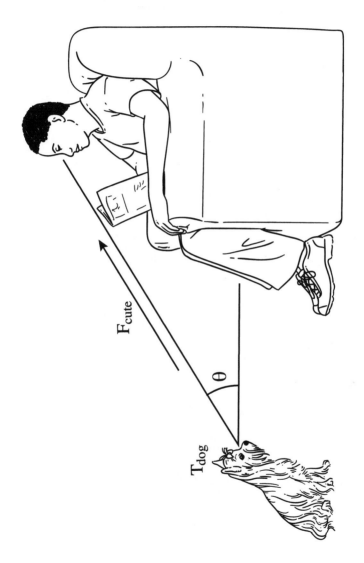

Fig. 56. Dog cutes human into submission.

YH-9. HELP YOUR HUMAN COOK DINNER

When helping you human with dinner remember that timing is everything. The best way to aid your human while cooking is by offering encouragement at just the right time. To ensure you get properly rewarded for your contribution time your encouragement using the following equations.

Time your bark to reach your human's ears at the precise moment the knife contacts the cutting board. Assuming the temperature in the kitchen is somewhat elevated from the heat of the stove, $T_k = 25°C$. At this temperature the speed of sound (v_s) is 346.3 m/s. Assume also your human moves the knife (v_c) at a rate of 0.1 m/s and lifts the knife each time to a height (d_c) of 0.085 m above the cutting board surface.

Let $t = 0$ at the beginning of the chop. Calculate the time it takes to complete 1 chop.

$$t_c = \frac{d_c}{v_c} = \frac{0.085\ m}{0.1\frac{m}{s}} = 0.85\ s$$

Now calculate the distance the sound must travel and the time it takes to travel from your mouth to your human's ear.

$$d_{BE} = \sqrt{(x_E - x_B)^2 + (y_E - y_B)^2 + (z_E - z_B)^2} = \sqrt{(0-3)^2 + (1.4-0)^2 + \left(0 - (-2)\right)^2}$$

$$d_{BE} = \sqrt{9 + 1.96 + 4} = 3.87\ m$$

$$t_s = \frac{d_{BE}}{v_s} = \frac{3.87\ m}{346.3\frac{m}{s}} = 0.011\ s$$

Now calculate the time you should initiate your bark (t_b) to ensure it reaches your human's ear at the correct moment.

$$t_b = t_c - t_s = 0.85\ s - 0.011\ s$$

$$t_b = 0.839\ s$$

Barking at this time after the initiation of a cut will ensure the knife will hurtle a freshly cute piece of food onto the floor for your consumption.

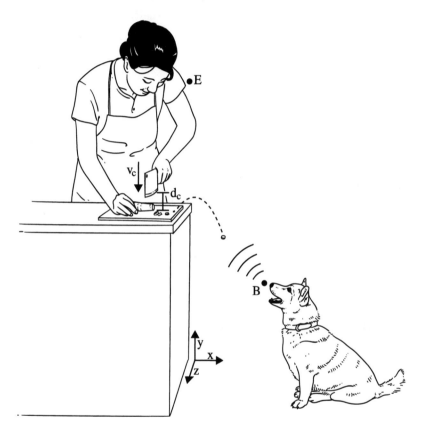

Fig. 57. Dog aids with meals with loud encouragement and consistent cleanup.

YH-10. ACCOMPANY YOUR HUMAN TO THE RESTROOM

Sometimes your human tries to sneak away and leave the house without you. To ensure your human stays in your presence you must accompany them everywhere they go. However, after realizing they are heading to the bathroom (also commonly referred to as the water closet, wc) you must determine whether or not you will follow. Use the following calculation. If $go_{wc} > 5$ then follow your human into the bathroom.

$$go_{wc} = \frac{k \left(\begin{array}{c} time\ last\ bath \\ was\ given \end{array} \right)}{\left(\begin{array}{c} time\ human\ last \\ went\ to\ wc \end{array} \right)^2} = \frac{k\ t_b}{t_{wc}^2}$$

$$k = 24 \frac{hr}{day} \times 60 \frac{min}{hr} = 1440 \frac{min}{day}$$

$$t_b = 12\ days$$

$$t_{wc} = 75\ mins$$

$$go_{wc} = \frac{1440 \frac{min}{day} \times 12\ days}{75\ mins^2} = 3.072$$

Since $go_{wc} > 5$ you can safely assume your human needs only to use the bathroom and is not trying to trick you into getting a bath.

or

or

Fig. 58. Dog calculates likelihood that human is entering bathroom to secretly escape.

YH-11. MASTER THE WET-DOG SHAKE

Whether it disgusts you or makes you feel like a puppy again, water makes every dog want to shake. And nothing makes you feel more gratified than sharing this wetness with your human. Determine the angular velocity to apply to the shake to make it most effective. Assume you can turn 95° in 0.5s.

$$\omega_{max} = \frac{95°}{0.5s} = 3.3 \; \frac{rad}{s}$$

To determine the amount of effort (% ω_{max}) to put into the shake use the following equation.

$$effort = \frac{Want\ to\ be\ dry + Want\ to\ get\ human\ wet}{2}$$

$$effort = \frac{0.43 + 0.99}{2} = 0.71$$

$$\omega_{eff} = effort \times \omega_{max} = 0.71 \times 3.3 = 2.34 \; \frac{rad}{s}$$

Now determine the maximum distance the water will spray. Use maximum x-direction velocity to calculate maximum x-direction travel.

$$v_{max} = r \times \omega_{eff} = 0.1524\ m \; \times 2.34 \frac{rad}{s} = 0.357 \frac{m}{s}$$

Calculate t using Δy

$$\Delta y = -0.5\ m \; ; \; v_{0y} = 0 \; ; \; a = -9.81 \frac{m}{s^2}$$

$$\Delta y = v_{0y}t + \frac{1}{2}at^2$$

$$-0.5m = 0 - \frac{1}{2} \times 9.81 \frac{m}{s^2} \times t^2$$

$$t^2 = \frac{2 \times 0.5m}{9.81 \frac{m}{s^2}}$$

$$t = 0.319s$$

Use t to calculate Δx.

$$\Delta x = v_{max}t = 0.357\frac{m}{s} \times 0.319s = 0.1138\ m$$

$$\Delta x = 11.38\ cm$$

So be sure to shake as close as possible to your human.

Fig. 59. Dog calculates effective distance and force necessary to share experience of being wet with human.

YH-12. MAKE THE MUDDY-DOG RUN

Your human's sense of smell is far less powerful than yours, so when you want to play a game of tag or hide-and-go-seek, it's best if you can leave a visible trail through the house. The Muddy Dog Run is a particularly interesting version of these games. Your objective: optimize your path's difficulty (P_d) for the best ratio of number of pieces of furniture you can stand on (f), number of obstacles you can pass—whether over, under, around, or through— with ease (O_e), and the total number of obstacles you must tackle on your run (O_t). You ultimately want the largest Mud Spread (MS) possible. If you can get to the end before your human, you win!

$$P_d = \frac{fO_e}{O_t}$$

$$MS = \frac{P_d(\# \ of \ shakes)}{d_{run}t_{run}}$$

To maximize the Mud Spread, you must choose a path with a high P_d with the lowest length and time.

Path 1:

$f_1 = 2$

$O_{e1} = 2$

$O_{t1} = 3$

$P_{d1} = 1.5$

$d_{run1} = 25m$

$t_{run1} = 30s$

$\# \ of \ shakes = 0$

$MS_1 = 0.002$

Path 2:

$f_2 = 1$

$O_{e2} = 3$

$O_{t2} = 3$

$P_{d2} = 1.0$

$d_{run2} = 20.4m$

$t_{run2} = 25s$

$\# \ of \ shakes = 2$

$MS_2 = 0.002$

Since $MS_2 > MS_1$, choose the second path as your route

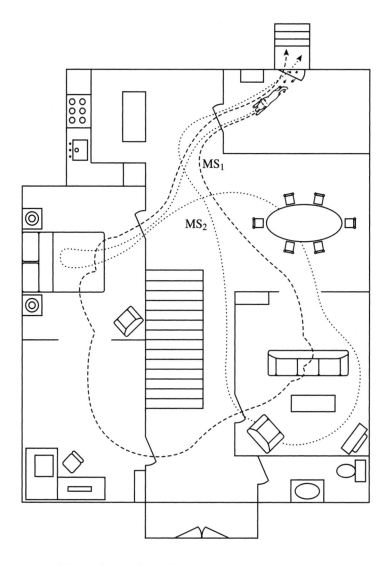

Fig. 60. Dog graciously leaves trail for human in game of indoor tag.

YH-13. PERFORM THE ITCHY-BUM SKID

There's no better way of showing your owner that you have a bowel problem than through the Itchy-Bum Skid—and if you do it well, you'll also relieve your own discomfort! Determine the force of your weight on the floor.

$$F_d = m_d g \; ; \; m_d = 13.6 \; kg$$

$$F_d = 13.6 \; kg \; \times 9.81 \frac{m}{s^2} = 133.5 \; N$$

Normal pulling force of your front paws is 1.5 your mass force.

$$F_{norm} = 1.5 \; F_d = 200.24 \; N$$

The Itch Motivator (much like the Treat Motivator) gives you a burst of strength for as long as your bum is itchy.

$$I_m = \frac{F_{norm}}{1.8} = \frac{200.24}{1.8} = 111.24 \; N$$

$$F_{max} = F_{norm} + I_m = 200.24 + 111.24 = 311.48 \; N$$

Now use the table to determine which floor surface you can scratch on.

Material 1	Material 2	M	Calculated Friction Force	Calculated Total Force
Dog bum	Wood	0.59	78.77	212.27
Dog bum	Carpet	1.20	160.20	293.70
Dog bum	Linoleum	0.32	42.72	176.22

Table 8. Motivation, Friction, and Force values as determined by Koleci's Laws

Scratching on the carpet will be the most satisfying.

Fig. 61. Dog indicates gastrointestinal irritation in classic
canine maneuver.

YH-14. PROTECT AND DEFEND YOUR HUMAN

You hear a noise! But what do you do?

Use the following table to determine your course of action.

Hazard Coefficient (H)	Action
0 > H > 10	Jump in front of your human and bark
10.1 > H > 20	Bark from behind human
20.1 > H > 30	Cower behind human
30.1 > H > 40	Run away and bark from at least 10m away
40.1 > H	Run away and don't come back, even if you're called

Table 9. Hazard Coeffecients and actions as set forth by the Society of Safe Canine Protocols.

This noise is accompanied by an ominous cloud *7m* away that has a perceived value of danger

(PVD) of 364.1.

$$H = \frac{PVD}{d} = \frac{364.1}{7\text{m}} = 52.01\frac{1}{\text{m}}$$

The noise and ominous cloud have a high enough Hazard Coefficient that you couldn't be

blamed for running away and not coming back when called. Until your human retreats from the

danger by another 2.1*m*, you shouldn't even bark at it!

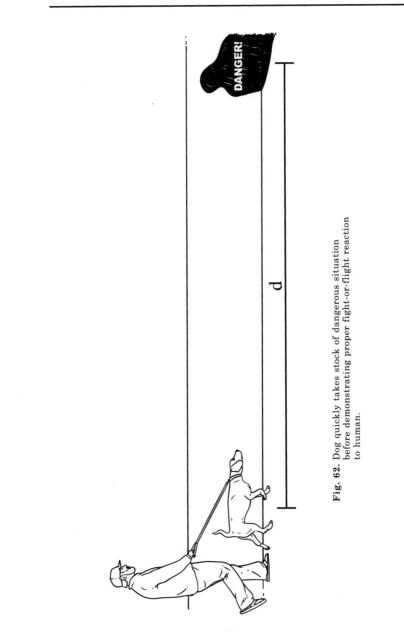

Fig. 62. Dog quickly takes stock of dangerous situation before demonstrating proper fight-or-flight reaction to human.

YH-15. DEMAND TO BE PET

Sometimes your human needs gentle reminders of how you two should be bonding. If you must

have attention, don't bark: just calculate the force needed to lift your human's hand

(m_{arm}=6.61kg) to the top of your head (m_{head}=1.13kg). You have to overcome static friction (μ_s

=0.8) created by the weight of your human's arm on your head.

$$F > \mu_s g(m_{arm} + m_{head}) = 0.8 \times 9.81 \frac{m}{s^2}(6.61kg + 1.13kg) = 60.74N$$

To continue sliding your head under his arm, you have to overcome the sliding friction (μ) of 0.6.

$$F = \mu g(m_{arm} + m_{head}) = 0.6 \times 9.81 \frac{m}{s^2}(6.61kg + 1.13kg) = 45.55N$$

If your human does not start scratching behind your ears when his hand gets to the top of your

head, consider the exercise failed; go ahead and bark until you get the attention you deserve!

Fig. 63. Dog physically asserts need for attention and love.

YH-16. INSIST ON BEING LEFT ALONE

There are times when your human gets on your last nerve or you are so tired that all you want to do is sleep. At these times you must determine the amount of heartbreak your human will suffer if you simply walk away and lie down alone.

Calculate the Heartbreak (Hb) using the following equation.

$$Hb = \frac{\left(\begin{array}{c} amount\ of \\ attention\ last \\ given\ to\ human \end{array}\right) \cdot \left[\left(\begin{array}{c} time\ lapse\ of \\ last\ attention\ given \\ to\ human \end{array}\right) + \left(\begin{array}{c} attention\ coefficeint \\ for\ last\ attention\ given, \\ in\ seconds \end{array}\right)\right]}{\left(\begin{array}{c} time\ lapse\ of \\ last\ snub \end{array}\right)^2}$$

$$Hb = \frac{\beta\ a_a(t_a + \alpha)}{t_{snub}^2}$$

The attention coefficient was empirically determined and values can be found in published tables. The last attention you gave your human was a greeting at the door when they came home. Given the following values calculate Heartbreak.

$\beta = 2.16 \times 10^7$

$a_a = 65\ s$

$t_a = 2\ hrs = 7200\ s$

$\alpha = 1240s$

$$t_{snub} = 1.5\ days = 1.3 \times 10^5 s$$

$$Hb = \frac{2.16 \times 10^7 \times 65\ s\ (7200\ s + 1240)}{(1.3 \times 10^5 s)^2}$$

$$Hb = 701.17$$

The Heartbreak Threshold Value of 1000 must not be exceeded or irreparable damage will be done to your relationship. Given this particular circumstance it is acceptable to snub your human without causing harm to your relationship.

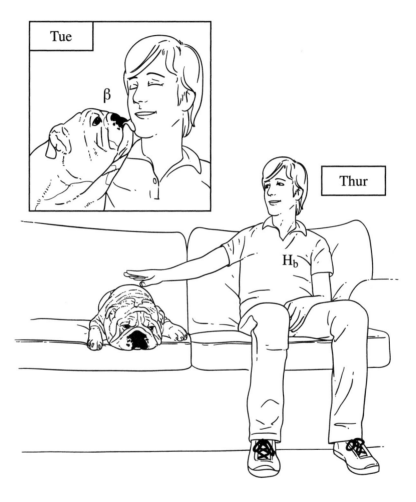

Fig. 64. Dog calculates impact of surly disposition on human's emotional state.

LESSONS IN THIS CHAPTER

FEATS OF GREATNESS

Many consider feats of greatness as reserved for those bred for the tasks. But canine physics will make all the difference. Height and weight are no barrier when the proper variables are accounted for. Overcoming gravity is easier when you correctly calculate the powerful pull of your prize. Your success will be assured when the most influential forces of all are leveraged in your favor. Whether you seek to impress the world at large or just your loyal human, these challenges could prove to bring the greatest rewards.

F-1. TAKE A JUMP

Possibly the most familiar obstacle on an agility course, this skill is useful in many situations both on and off the field. There is no force resisting horizontal motion. Find the velocity (v) at which you need to launch to achieve a vertical range(h) of 0.35m with a jump angle (θ) of 45°, assuming $v_x = v \cos \theta$ and $v_y = v \sin \theta$. Use the equations of motion to calculate velocity.

$$v = \sqrt{\frac{2gh}{\sin^2 \theta}} = \sqrt{\frac{2 \times 9.81 \frac{m}{s^2} \times 0.35 \, m}{\sin^2 45°}} = 3.71 \, \frac{m}{s}$$

Calculate the time spent in your jump, then calculate the horizontal range (d) of your jump:

$$t = 2\left(\frac{v - v_i}{g}\right) = 2\left(\frac{3.71 \frac{m}{s} - 0}{9.81 \frac{m}{s^2}}\right) = 0.76 \, s$$

$$d = \frac{1}{2}v \, \cos \theta \, t = \frac{1}{2} \times 3.71 \frac{m}{s} \times \cos 45° \cdot 0.76 \, s = 1.00 \, m$$

Find the work (W) needed to complete the jump if you weigh 20kg.

$$W = Fd = (ma)d = (20kg)\left(9.81 \frac{m}{s^2}\right)(1.00 \, m) = 196.2 \, J$$

To determine your enjoyment factor (E) for the jump, especially on the agility course, complete the following calculation, letting t stand for the number of treats you'll be given for completion, n for the number of times you've already completed jumps when asked, I for interest (which is also expressed as n/25).

$$E = \frac{3\left(\frac{t^t}{T}\right)}{Wn} = \frac{75t^t}{n} \cdot \frac{1}{Wn} = \frac{75t^t}{Wn^2}$$

Early in the training session (n is small) your E will be higher:

$$E = \frac{75 \cdot 2^2}{196.2 \, J \cdot 1^2} = 1.53$$

Later, as n gets larger, you may find it hard to be motivated by the same number of treats:

$$E = \frac{75 \cdot 2^2}{196.2 \, J \cdot 6^2} = 0.042$$

$$E = \frac{75 \cdot 4^4}{196.2 \, J \cdot 6^2} = 2.72$$

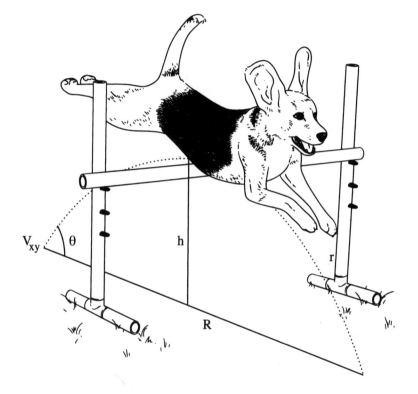

Fig. 65. Dog calculates properties of jump and amount of
treats needed to repeat it.

F-2. RUN THE A-FRAME

The A-Frame is a favorite of long-limbed dogs, but even shorter breeds can take on the $6ft$ obstacle. This set of calculations for the work necessary to climb the A Frame (W_f) assumes a spatially invariant force, a mass of $13.6kg$, constant speed, and mastery of balance.

$$v = 11 \, \frac{m}{s}$$

$$W_f = Force \times distance$$

To accomplish the feat, you must overcome the force (F) component of gravity along the slope.

$$F = mg \times \cos{^\theta/_2} = 13.6kg \times 9.81 \frac{m}{s^2} \times \cos 48 = 85.41 \, N$$

Distance (d/2): length of slope going up

$$^d/_2 = 2.1 \, m$$

Therefore,

$$W_f = 85.41 \, N \times \; 2.1 \, m = 179.35 \, J$$

W_a: how tasty treat appears

$$W_a = F_a n$$

n: number of expected treats

F_a: Force of treat's appeal

$$F_a = my$$

m: treat's mass

y: how yummy treat smells

If $\qquad W_a > W_f \qquad$ Run over A frame

If $\qquad W_a < W_f \qquad$ Treat is not worth effort. Take Route β instead

If $\qquad W_a = W_f \qquad$ Bite your tail! There's just no good answer. . . .

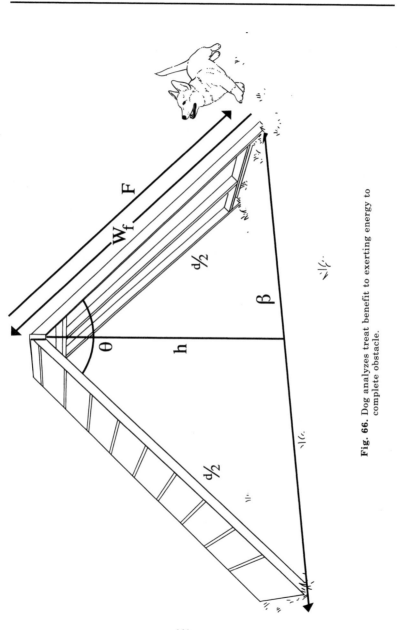

Fig. 66. Dog analyzes treat benefit to exerting energy to complete obstacle.

F-3. MASTER THE SEESAW

The seesaw is more intimidating than your human seems to think it is. Not only does it move whether you do or not, it produces a sound thud when its far end hits the ground. As you've learned, *F=ma*. You can now calculate how hard the seesaw will hit the ground when you're on it and prepare yourself for the unpleasant shock.

Use the equation of motion to determine your acceleration.

$$v^2 = u^2 + 2at$$

but your initial velocity is zero, therefore

$$a = \frac{v^2}{2t}$$

Potential energy lost between the top and bottom of the fall will all be converted to kinetic energy, assuming no work is done by non-conservative forces.

$$\Delta P_e = \Delta K_e$$

$$\Delta P_e = mg\Delta h = \frac{1}{2}mv^2 = \Delta K_e$$

$$\Delta P_e = 30kg \times 9.81 \frac{m}{s^2} \times 0.08m = 23.54\,J = \Delta K_e$$

$$\Delta K_e = \frac{1}{2}mv^2 = 23.54\,J$$

$$v = \sqrt{\frac{23.54J \times 2}{30kg}} = 1.25\frac{m}{s}$$

With this velocity, acceleration becomes

$$a = \frac{1.25^2}{2 \times 0.08} = 9.77\frac{m}{s^2}$$

And you will hit the ground with a force:

$$F = ma = 30kg \times 9.77\frac{m}{s^2} = 293.1\,N$$

While you may worry that this will be too jarring a force to safely stay on the obstacle, remember that it would take nearly twice that force to launch you off of the seesaw. A dog without the leisure of long legs to absorb the shock can rest assured that while it may not be a pleasant experience, safety shouldn't be a concern.

Fig. 67. Dog prepares self for movement of unstable obstacle.

F-4. RUN THROUGH AN AGILITY TUNNEL

When your human wants you to run through a dark tunnel without them you must decide for yourself the level of danger (Da_{nger}) involved. Compare the level of danger with the scrumptiousness (Sc_{rumpt}) of the treat your human is currently in possession of. If $Sc_{rumpt} > Da_{nger}$ then proceed through the tunnel. If, however, $Sc_{rumpt} < Da_{nger}$ then fight with all your might not to go through.

$$Da_{nger} = \left(\begin{array}{c} length \\ of\ tunnel \end{array}\right) \left[\frac{\left(\begin{array}{c} brightness \\ outside\ tunnel \end{array}\right)}{\left(\begin{array}{c} brightness \\ in\ tunnel \end{array}\right)} - \left(\begin{array}{c} previous\ number \\ of\ times\ through \\ tunnel \end{array}\right)\right] = l_t\left(\frac{b_o}{b_i} - n\right)$$

Brightness is expressed in freenclear units (fc). Assuming a sunny day with minimal cloud cover and a dark colored agility tunnel we have the following values.

$$l_t = 1.4\ m\ ;\ b_o = 8,000\ fc\ ;\ b_i = 60\ fc\ ;\ n = 0$$

$$Da_{nger} = 1.4\ m\ \cdot \left(\frac{8000\ fc}{60\ fc} - 0\right) = 186.67\ m$$

Scrumptiousness values of certain commonly found treats have been empirically determined. Use the published tables to find the scrumptiousness of the chicken your human currently possesses. You saw the piece of chicken has a volume of approximately $1\ cm^3$.

Treat	Sc_{rumpt}
Bacon (1 strip)	1×10^5
Chicken (whole breast)	Too large to measure
Chicken (~125 cm³)	1×10^5
Chicken (~27 cm³)	5000
Chicken (~1 cm³)	150

Table 10. Sc_rumpt values found in *Scamp's Little Book of Food Physics*

Since $Sc_{rumpt} < Da_{nger}$ hold out for more treats. When your human pulls out another treat the scrumptiousness of that treat must be added to the original scrumptiousness. Another piece of chicken of the same approximate size will be sufficient.

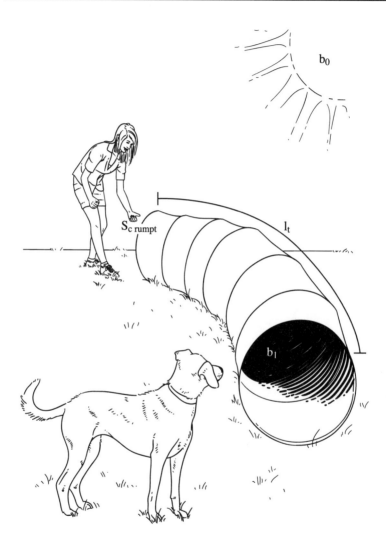

Fig. 68. Dog compares danger of dark tunnel to size of reward for obstacle completion.

F-5. HERD APPROPRIATELY SIZED ANIMALS

Whether for work or sport, herding is a classic partnership between humans, canines, and herd animals. If you are not a herder by nature or trade, pay close attention to the delicate balance between work and play. Calculate the time spent herding by taking the difference of the Enjoyment Factor (E) and the Exertion Quotient (χ).

$$t_H = E - \chi$$

$$E = \frac{m_{animal}}{m_{dog}} \times \frac{percieved\ difficulty}{(\#\ times\ stepped\ on + 1) \times (\#\ times\ kicked + 1)}$$

$$\chi = \left(\frac{s_{animal}}{s_{dog}} \times \#\ of\ animals\right) + \frac{percieved\ difficulty}{times\ herded\ before + 1}$$

Given the following values, calculate the time you'll spend herding.

$$m_{sheep} = 68.03kg$$

$$m_{dog} = 36.28kg$$

$$stepped\ on = 0$$

$$kicks = 3$$

$$percieved\ difficulty = 1000$$

$$s_{sheep} = 12.98\frac{m}{s}$$

$$s_{dog} = 13.39\frac{m}{s}$$

$$\#\ sheep = 25$$

$$times\ herded\ before = 2$$

$$E = \frac{68.03kg}{36.28kg} \times \frac{1000}{1 \times 4} = 468.78\ s$$

$$\chi = \left(\frac{12.98\frac{m}{s}}{13.39\frac{m}{s}} \times 25\right) + \frac{1000}{3} = 357.53s$$

$$t_H = 468.78\ s - 357.53s = 111.25s$$

You should give this a cautious go for a few minutes. Make sure to recalculate if your experience improves the perceived difficulty drastically.

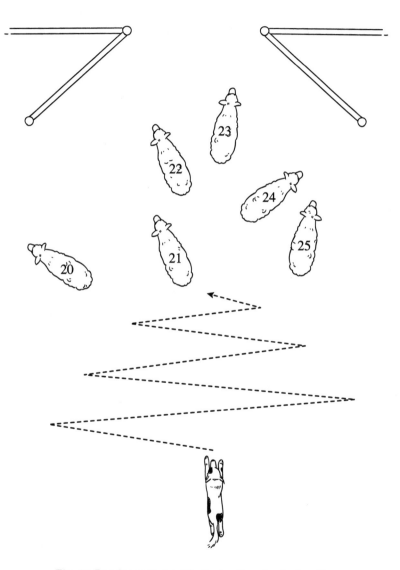

Fig. 69. Dog demonstrates effective herding of animals with proper breed-to-target size ratio.

F-6. HERD INAPPROPRIATELY SIZED ANIMALS

Some dogs have the confidence and skill to pursue game far above their size class. This gives the course a particular thrill for some breeds. If you are neither experienced in herding nor bred for this task, attempt to avoid this lesson until you have at least progressed to 10 minute bouts based on your calculations in F-4. Herd appropriately sized animals.

$$t_H = E - \chi$$

$$E = \frac{m_{animal}}{m_{dog}} \times \frac{percieved\ difficulty}{(\#\ times\ stepped\ on + 1) \times (\#\ times\ kicked + 1)}$$

$$\chi = \left(\frac{s_{animal}}{s_{dog}} \times \#\ of\ animals\right) + \frac{percieved\ difficulty}{times\ herded\ before + 1}$$

Now, run the calculations with the following variables

$$m_{cow} = 635.02kg$$

$$m_{dog} = 13.60kg$$

$$stepped\ on = 3$$

$$kicks = 5$$

$$percieved\ difficulty = 1500$$

$$s_{cow} = 7.59\frac{m}{s}$$

$$s_{dog} = 10.53\frac{m}{s}$$

$$\#\ cows = 25$$

$$times\ herded\ before = 6$$

$$E = \frac{635.02kg}{13.60kg} \times \frac{1500}{4 \times 6} = 7{,}202.48\ s$$

$$\chi = \left(\frac{7.59\frac{m}{s}}{10.53\frac{m}{s}} \times 25\right) + \frac{1500}{6} = 268.01s$$

$$t_H = 7{,}202.48\ s - 268.01s = 6{,}934.47s$$

The difference in speed in this situation would keep you running for hours—literally! A faster herd animal would not be a wise choice in this scenario.

Fig. 70. Dog demonstrates reckless herding of animals vastly larger than assumed proper.

F-7. DUCK HUNT

Bird hunting combines the skills you learned in fetch in a much more pleasant setting with better motivators!

Here, the duck is flying horizontally at a velocity of 8m/s at a height of 3m. There is no wind and air resistance is negligible, therefore, there is no force opposing horizontal motion. Your human shoots at a height of 2m with an angle (θ) of 40°. The bullet hits the duck almost instantaneously. At this point, the duck will undergo projectile motion until it hits the ground. Calculate how far it will travel before it hits the ground and how much energy you will spend getting to the duck the second it hits.

At moment of impact with bullet, duck is at its maximum height (h_{max}) of 36m. Let t_{fall} stand for the time it takes for the duck to fall from h_{max} to ground. The duck's speed (u_1) at h_{max} is 0m/s.

$$h_{max} = u_1 t_{fall} + 0.5g(t_{fall})^2$$

$$35\,m = 0\frac{m}{s} + 0.5s \times 9.81\frac{m}{s^2} \times (t_{fall})^2$$

$$t_{fall} = \sqrt{\frac{35\,m}{0.5 \times 9.81\frac{m}{s^2}}} = 2.67s$$

x_1: horizontal distance covered by duck

$$x_1 = speed\ of\ duck \times t_{fall} = 8\frac{m}{s} \times 2.67\,s = 21.37\,m$$

x_2: horizontal separation of duck from human when it gets hit

$$x_2 = \frac{h_{max} - h_{human}}{\tan 40} = \frac{35\,m - 2\,m}{\tan 40} = 39.33\,m$$

x_{total}: total distance between human and point of impact of duck with ground

$$x_{total} = x_1 + x_2 = 21.37\,m + 39.33\,m = 60.7\,m$$

E: energy spent to run to duck as soon as it hits the ground

$$E = mad$$

$$a = \frac{x_{total} - u_1 t_{fall}}{\frac{1}{2}(t_{fall})^2} = \frac{60.7\ m - 0\ m}{0.5(2.67)^2\ s^2} = 17.03\ m/s^2$$

$$E = mad = 15\ kg \times 17.03\frac{m}{s^2} \times 60.7\ m = 15{,}505.2\ J$$

As food calorie is equal to 4180 Joules, 15,502.2 J is equal to 3.71 Food Calories or less than a stick of bubble gum! It's no wonder you can do this all day!

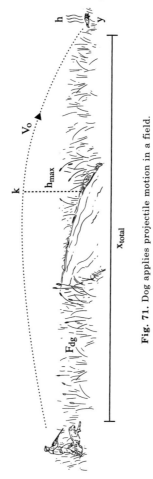

Fig. 71. Dog applies projectile motion in a field.

F-8. PULL A SLED

Sled dogs are majestic and respected, but not everyone was built for the sport. Before you undertake the task of pulling anything—especially little humans—make sure you're up to the job!

First, calculate the force necessary to pull the wooden sled on icy snow

$$F_{sled} = \mu(m_{k1} + m_{k2} + m_{sled})g$$

$$m_{k1} = 31.75kg$$

$$m_{k2} = 40.12kg$$

$$m_{sled} = 5kg$$

$$\mu = 0.1$$

$$F_{sled} = 0.1 \times (31.75kg + 40.12k + 5kg) \times 9.81\frac{m}{s^2} = 75.41N$$

Calculate your pull force (F_{dog}). Assume your pull force is equal to your mass-force.

$$m_{dog} = 13.6kg$$

$$F_{dog} = mg = 13.6kg \times 9.81\frac{m}{s^2} = 133.5N$$

Determine the ratio of F_{sled} to F_{dog}.

$$\frac{F_{sled}}{F_{dog}} = \frac{75.41N}{133.5N} = 0.56$$

Since the ratio of F_{sled} to F_{dog} is > 0.5, you are convinced that the sled will just be too heavy for your comfort. Instead, sit in the sled and wait for one of the children to pull.

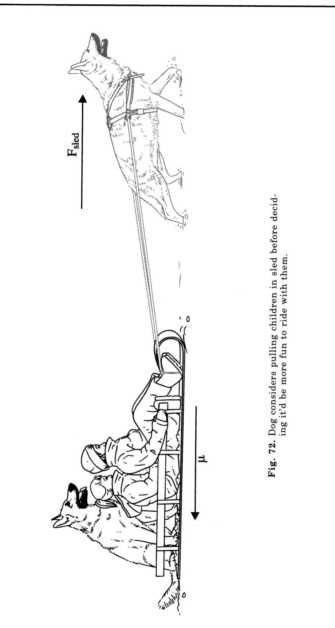

Fig. 72. Dog considers pulling children in sled before deciding it'd be more fun to ride with them.

F-9. HIKE A MOUNTAIN

Yet another classic canine sport, hiking requires stamina beyond most of your previous lessons. After all, you will be pulling your owner up the mountain while you both carry packs, and you're likely to cover three times the distance as your human because you are compelled to run the trail three times while he walks it once. But be aware: your excitement could drastically increase the work you do.

$$W = F\Delta d$$

$$F = \left[m_d + m_{pd} + \frac{1}{5}(m_h + m_{ph}) \right] g$$

$$d = 600m$$

$$m_d = 30kg$$

$$m_{pd} = \frac{1}{3}m_d = 10kg$$

$$\Delta d_d = 3d = 1800m$$

$$m_h = 75kg$$

$$m_{ph} = \frac{1}{3}m_h = 25kg$$

$$F = \left[30kg + 10kg + \frac{1}{5}(75kg + 25kg) \right] 9.81\frac{m}{s^2} = 568.98N$$

$$W_d = 568.98N \times 1800m = 1.02MNm$$

Compare to the work done by your human.

$$W_h = F\Delta d = (75 + 25) \times 9.81\frac{m}{s^2} \times 600m = 0.58MNm$$

You're doing approximately two times the work your human is doing!

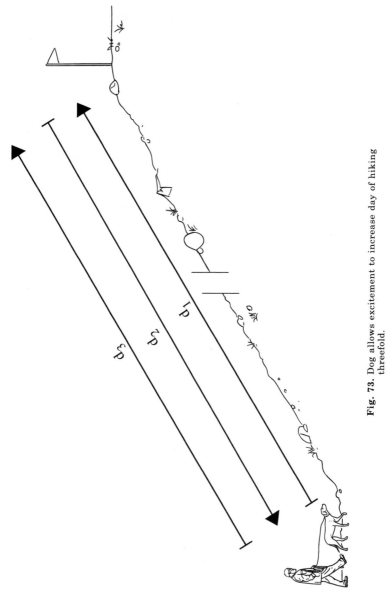

Fig. 73. Dog allows excitement to increase day of hiking threefold.

F-10. DIVE INTO WATER

Your toy has fallen into the pool (what better place for it to be?), and an opportune moment presents itself. If you use projectile motion to launch yourself correctly, you'll be able to jump into a wave trough, create the biggest wave possible, and in doing so attempt to get the cat on the other side wet. You want to jump 1.75m (d_1) to successfully get the toy back. You know that the edge of the pool is above the water level by 0.2m (h). Calculate how much time you need to wait to jump.

Knowing that the frequency of waves (f) is 0.4 wave per second (or 0.4 Hz) and that the distance (λ) between 2 consecutive wave troughs is 0.35m will allow you to calculate for v_{wave}, the velocity of the wave:

$$v_{wave} = f\lambda = 0.4\ Hz \times 0.35\ m = 0.14\ m/s$$

The spot into which you want to jump into is located 2.25m (d_2)from cat's side of pool. Find the time that wave trough will take to travel 2.25m.

$$t_{wave} = \frac{distance}{v_{wave}} = \frac{2.25\ m}{0.14\ m/s} = 16.1\ s$$

You don't want the cat to see through your plan, so you wait exactly 15s, leaving yourself 1.1s to make the jump. Determine the angle and speed at which you need

$$y = (u\sin\theta)t - 0.5gt^2$$

y: height of dog at any time. At 1.1 seconds, dog needs to have fallen 0.2m to be in the water

t: time (1.1s)

u: speed of jump

θ: angle of jump

$$-0.2 = (u \sin \theta)(1.1 \, s) - 0.5 \times 9.81 \frac{m}{s^2} \times (1.1 \, s)^2$$

$$u \sin \theta = 5.20$$

The horizontal displacement of the dog is given by

$$u \cos \theta = \frac{x}{t} = \frac{1.75m}{1.1s} = 1.59$$

Combining the two equations yields

$$\frac{u \sin \theta}{u \cos \theta} = \tan \theta = \frac{5.20}{1.59} = 3.26$$

$$\theta = 73^0$$

To find the speed along direction of jump (u)

$$u \cos \theta = 1.5 \frac{m}{s} \quad (horizontal \; speed)$$

$$u = \frac{1.59}{\cos 73^0} = 5.43 \; m/s$$

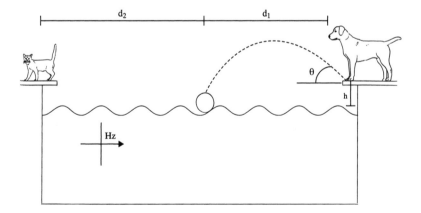

Fig. 74. Dog combines well-calculated dive with plot to
upset archenemy.

F-11. SWIM ACROSS A POND

You could swim all day if it weren't for drag. If you can calculate the drag of water on fur coat, you'll know how much harder you'll have to work.

$$F_d = \frac{1}{2}\rho u^2 C_d A$$

ρ: mass density of water, 998.2 kg/m^3

u: constant velocity relative to water, 1.39 m/s

A: cross-sectional area of the dog (assuming a sphere), πr^2

C_d: drag coefficient (assuming a half sphere), 0.42

$$A = \pi \times (0.25\ m)^2 = 0.20\ m^2$$

$$F_d = \frac{1}{2} \times 998.2\ \frac{kg}{m^3} \times 1.39^2 \frac{m^2}{s^2} \times 0.42 \times 0.20\ m^2$$

$$F_d = 81.00\ N$$

Total work needed to swim to dock:

$$W = F_d \times distance$$

$$W = 81.00\ N \times 860\ m = 69{,}661.83\ J$$

For every 1 Joule (J) there are .000239 kilocalories (kcal). Therefore, swimming to the boat expends,

$$69{,}661.83\ J \times .000239\ \frac{kcal}{J} = 16.65\ kcal$$

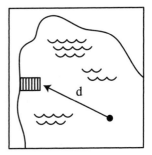

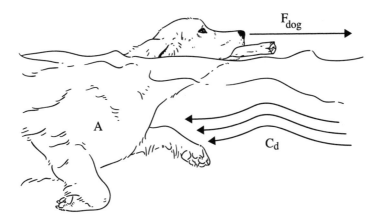

Fig. 75. Dog accounts for drag and its impact on an otherwise easy turn about the lake.

F-12. WIN A SHOW RIBBON

You are surrounded by people and dogs, but you're being told to stay. *Stay.* Your owner may not

have a treat in his pocket, but you're pretty sure the poodle's owner does and you're confident

that you are cute enough to win her over . . . but no, you intend to attempt pleasing your own

human first. Calculate the time you can bear stand still using the following formula.

$$t_{ss} = \frac{\left(\begin{array}{c}\text{time your human}\\\text{spent training you}\end{array}\right) + \left(\begin{array}{c}\text{love of}\\\text{your human}\end{array}\right)}{3600\left(\begin{array}{c}\text{Number of distractions}\\\text{currently in your}\\\text{line of sight}\end{array}\right)} = \frac{t_{train} \cdot Lv}{3600 \cdot D}$$

As love of your human increases, time able to stand still increases.

$$Lv = 38 \quad ; \quad t_{train} = 100 \; hrs \quad ; \quad D = 1027$$

$$t_{ss} = \frac{100 \times 38}{3600 \times 1027} = 1.028 \times 10^{-3} \; hrs$$

$$t_{ss} = 3.7 \; seconds$$

Your human will just have to understand that you just aren't interested in beauty contests.

Fig. 76. Dog attempts to steel self against nearly innumerable distractions in the show ring.

F-13. WIN A DANCE CONTEST

You will be sure to win any dance contest with this classic Waltz step.

Calculate the Work required to complete one box step. Assume a square dance box with dimension, $l = 0.25\ m$. The equation for work is:

$$W = F\,d = m\,g\,d$$

Even though you are making 6 steps you only move your entire body twice. Therefore the total work required is equal to

$$W = 2\,m\,g\,d_{bias}$$

Given

$$m = 16.4\ kg\ ;\ g = 9.81\frac{m}{s^2}\ ;\ l = 0.25\ m$$

Calculate d_{bias} then W.

For a square:

$$d_{bias} = \sqrt{2l^2} = \sqrt{2 \times (0.25\ m)^2}$$

$$d_{bias} = 0.35\ m$$

$$W = 2 \times 16.4\ kg \times 9.81\frac{m}{s^2} \cdot 0.35\ m$$

$$W = 112.62\ J$$

This step requires a fairly small amount of Work and will be sure to bring big rewards.

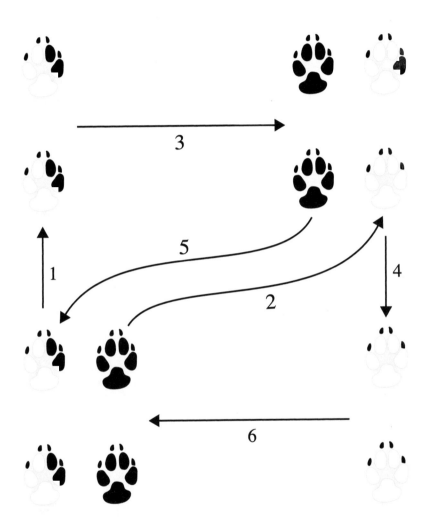

Fig. 77. Dog learns classic Waltz to charm talent show judges.

F-14. TAKE DOWN A CRIMINAL

By the time you see the perp in front of you, there's never much time to think. Do the math ahead of time to ensure your success! Calculate the force you need to make the criminal fall. Criminal will be assumed to be standing straight up, with his feet together, creating the hinge will be at his feet.

Assume criminal is standing straight up, with his feet together, creating the hinge at his feet.

F_{thigh}: 264 N

h_{thigh}: 0.45 m

F_{torso}: 157 N

h_{torso}: 1.2 m

F_{head}: 58 N

h_{head}: 1.84m

Those three forces are acting in a horizontal direction producing clockwise moment

$$Moment = \Sigma(Force \times Perpendicular\ distance)$$

$$Moment = (264 \times 0.45) + \ (157 \times 1.2) \times (58 \times 1.84)$$

$$Moment = 367.04\ Nm$$

To take criminal down, you have to create a moment of more than 367.04 Nm. The minimum force that you have to apply on the criminal at his torso is

$$367.04\ Nm = F_{dog} \times 1.2m$$

$$F_{dog} = \frac{367.04}{1.2} = 305.87\ N$$

This force has to be applied in the horizontal direction. However, dog will be jumping from the ground and the force will be at an angle to the horizontal. That angle is

$$\tan \theta = \frac{h_{torso}}{distance\ that\ dog\ will\ jump\ from}$$

$$\tan \theta = \frac{1.2\ m}{1\ m}$$

$$\theta = 50.2\ degrees$$

The horizontal component of the force equals 305.87 N. The actual force is

$$F_{actual} \cos 50.2 = 305.87\ N$$

$$F_{actual} = 477.8\ N$$

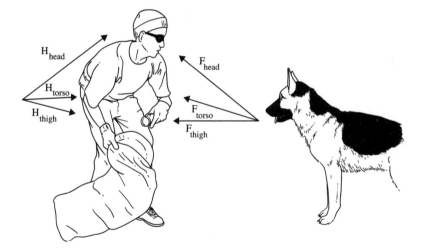

Fig. 78. Dog calculates force necessary to immobilize a villain.

F-15. FIND THE PERFECT SPOT TO LAY DOWN

Finding the perfect spot to lie in requires a delicate balance of variables. Spot value is not intuitive, a spot with a minimum spot value is preferred. In order to minimize the spot value (S) you must choose wisely.

$$S = \frac{2 \begin{pmatrix} distance\ from \\ favorite\ human \end{pmatrix} \times \begin{pmatrix} current\ distance \\ from\ spot \end{pmatrix} + \frac{1}{4\pi} \begin{pmatrix} distance\ from \\ heat\ source\ other \\ than\ human \end{pmatrix}^2}{\begin{pmatrix} Comfiness\ factor \\ of\ possible\ spot \end{pmatrix}}$$

$$S = \frac{2 d_{hu} d_s + \frac{1}{4\pi} d_{he}^2}{C}$$

Look up the Comfiness factor from published tables; part of these tables are represented in YH-5. Keep human's bed warm. Compare two potential spots and choose the one with the lowest Spot value.

Spot 1

$$d_{hu} = 0.2\ m\ ;\ d_s = 2.1\ m\ ;\ d_{he} = 3.41\ m\ ;\ C = 8.4$$

$$S_1 = \frac{2 \times 0.2\ m \times 2.1\ m + \frac{1}{4\pi} \times (3.41\ m)^2}{8.4}$$

$$S_1 = 0.21$$

Spot 2

$$d_{hu} = 1.8\ m\ ;\ d_s = 1.73\ m\ ;\ d_{he} = 0.52\ m\ ;\ C = 3.5$$

$$S_2 = \frac{2 \times 1.8\ m \times 1.73\ m + \frac{1}{4\pi} \times (0.52\ m)^2}{3.5}$$

$$S_2 = 1.79$$

Since $S_1 = 0.21 \ll S_2 = 1.79$, Spot 1 s your best choice.

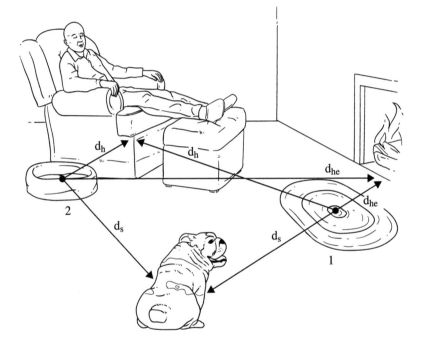

Fig. 79. Dog eliminates need to spin in precisely 4.7 circles to prime resting place by factoring in Comfiness Factor and distance to human.

F-16. RESCUE TIMMY FROM THE WELL

No dog can deny the innate desire to be a hero. Collies may have had a monopoly on the silver screen, but every dog is capable of saving the day! And you don't even need the communication skills to ask grandpa for help!

Should Timmy—or Tommy or Billy or Jimmy or any local child—fall down a well, simply analyze the pulley system to determine the work you'll need to do to save him or her. In this case, there are 5 sections (N). As you'll be pulling down, your direction of pull will have a value of -1. Calculate your mechanical advantage (MA).

$$MA = N + direction\ of\ pull = 5 - 1 = 4$$

Therefore the amount of Timmy's weight you'll need to pull (Fr) is

$$Fr = \left(\frac{1}{MA}\right) = \frac{1}{4}$$

Now find Timmy's downward force (F_d) and the force (F) needed to save Timmy.

$$F_d = mg = 9.81\frac{m}{s^2} \times 45kg = 441.41N$$

$$F = Fr \times F_d = \frac{1}{4}441.45N = 119.36N$$

The average work required to pull Timmy from the well by pulling him 3.05m upward (d_l)will then be

$$W = Fd_l = 119.36N \times 3.05m = 336.61J$$

As any movie-friendly dog knows, a 25s rescue both prolongs viewers suspense over Timmy's fate and is a safe for the child and yourself. Calculate the average power (P) this requires.

$$P = \frac{W}{t} = \frac{336.61J}{25s} = 13.46\ Watts$$

Your reward can be found with the Power of Love Factor (P_L).

$$P_L = 0.7\frac{hugs}{Watt}P = 0.7\frac{hugs}{Watt} \times 13.46Watts = 9.42\ hugs$$

Fig. 80. Dog shows up Hollywood actors with knowledge of
pulley systems and real-world physics of dramatic
timing.

GLOSSARY

a: acceleration, often.

d: distance, often. Also disruptiveness.

E: see Enjoyment factor.

ED: see Emotional Damage factor.

Emotional Damage Factor: the numeric value of your human's negative reaction to an action.

Enjoyment Factor: the numeric value of your positive emotional reaction to an action.

Equation of Motion: $s^2 = u^2 + 2at$

F: see Force.

F_f: Force of static friction.

Force: $F = ma$

g: see Gravity.

Gravity: $9.81N$

H: see Hazard Coefficient

Hazard Coefficient: the ratio of perceived danger to distance.

indoor relief: $r = visibility + smell\ retention + absorption\ rate - (distance)(laziness)$

l: see laziness factor.

Law of Cosines: $c^2 = a^2 + b^2 - 2abcos\theta$

Laziness factor: the scientifically defined rate of lethargy acting upon a dog in any given situation, according Newton's First and Second Laws of Canine Motion. Holds a value of 0 to 10, except in extreme situations including states of frap (medical records of an unidentified Jack Russell puppy dipped to -9.74) and fireside naps (a 97 year-old Newfoundland was able to reach 21.83; higher rates have been fatal). Its units are considered to be the inverse of units of measure.

m: mass.

Newton's Laws of Canine Motion :

1.   A dog at rest will stay at rest unless acted upon by an external force of nature greater than the force of laziness. A dog in motion will stay in motion until he reaches the end of the leash.

2.   A dog of mass, m, subject to a force, Treat, undergoes an acceleration, Run, having the same direction as the force and a magnitude directly proportional to the force and inversely proportional to its mass.

3.   For every dog, there is an equal and opposite human.

OhMyGod : the OhMyGod value superceeds the Enjoyment (E) factor by a power of 10^9

R: see Range.

r: traditionally radius; also see Revenge magnitude.

radius: the distance between the center of a circle or sphere and its circumference.

Range: $R = \dfrac{u^2 \sin 2\theta}{g}$

PHYSICS FOR DOGS

Revenge magnitude: the impact of an act performed to raise another's awareness of a problematic situation. Some common formulas solve for magnitude of indoor relief, indoor excrement, and vomit.

S: see Stinks units.

s: speed, unless expressing a unit, then seconds.

s2: see equation of motion.

Stinks units: the measurement of an object's property of smell (commonly, smelliness) given in units of mp/mm³. Named after the renowned excrementologist Jorriah P. Stinks.

Speed: $s = \frac{d}{t}$

t: time.

τ: see Trouble factor.

Treat Motivator: a force that varies based on size, taste, and preference. Field tests show that a treat considered normal in size and rarity by a dog usually has a value of 0.3.

Treat Strength Multiplier: a coefficient of 5.5. Field tests show that when restrained from reaching a treat (or an object perceived as a treat), a dog's normal pulling strength will increase by the TSM.

Trouble Factor: impact of an action upon your human's daily activities, expressed in a percentage that those activities must change.

W: see Work.

Work: $W = Fd$

About the Authors

John-Andrew Sandbrook is a senior mathematical sciences and computer science major at Worcester Polytechnic Institute. As a lifelong dog owner he's seen his fair share of canine physics feats—and fails! Sandbrook once lived next door to a Pit Bull who could clear a six-foot fence and fell for a Giant Schnauzer puppy that insisted he was a lap dog. Sandbrook's own dogs were similarly talented: his parents' Shepherd-Husky once caught a cat (and didn't know what to do with it), his Sheltie herded people more often than sheep, and his sister's Shih Tzu made valiant attempts at defying gravity when begging for popcorn. These and other dogs' stories convinced Sandbrook a true physics text needed to be written for canines worldwide. He lives in Worcester, Massachusetts.

Dara Flynn, MS received her Bachelor of Science in Mechanical Engineering and her Master of Science in Materials Science from Worcester Polytechnic Institute. The proud owner of a physics-ally inclined Doberman, Flynn has survived many of these scenarios on the wrong side of a clever canine. From several strategic puking incidents and a laughable attempt at a sled pull to valiant conquests of ants and cowardly shivers at the smallest sign of thunder, Flynn observed and conducted countless dog years of field experiments and lab trials before undertaking coauthorship of this book. She lives in Brockton, Massachusetts.

About the Technical Editor

Carolann Koleci received her Bachelor of Science in Physics from the University at Albany, State University of New York. She continued her education at Brown University, where she completed two Masters of Science in Physics and Mechanical Engineering and her PhD in Physics Education. Her dissertation was entitled *Inquiry Based Problem Solving in Introductory Physics*. She is a member of AAPT, AERA, and the American Physical Society: Forum on Physics Education. Koleci is currently an Adjunct Assistant Professor and Director of Physics Education at Worcester Polytechnic Institute. She currently resides in Albany, NY.

About the Foreword Writer

Pepper Sandbrook-Flynn, PhD, is a Pembroke Welsh Corgi and a well-regarded master of canine physics, despite her short stature. An agility dog by trade, she earned her People Handling Degree from Ruffgurrs University at only six weeks old. Her dissertation, entitled *Coercion at Any Size*, detailed her work combining psychology and mechanics to convince her owner to break every rule he'd set for her the moment he brought her home. She began postgraduate work in agility in 2009. Sandbrook-Flynn accounts for her success, in part, the counter-balance of her naturally long tail which defies breed standards. She lives with her owners in Brockton, Massachusetts.